HOW TO HAVE A
BETTER LIFE

GOD'S WISDOM FROM THE BOOK OF PROVERBS IN 175 DAILY DEVOTIONS

BRENTON COX

WESTBOW
PRESS®
A DIVISION OF THOMAS NELSON
& ZONDERVAN

"Voice of Truth," written by John Mark Hall and Steven Curtis Chapman. Copyright 2103 Be Essential Songs (BMI) (admin at EssentialMusicPublishing.com.) All rights reserved. Used by permission.

This book is a work of non-fiction. Unless otherwise noted, the author and the publisher make no explicit guarantees as to the accuracy of the information contained in this book and in some cases, names of people and places have been altered to protect their privacy.

WestBow Press books may be ordered through booksellers or by contacting:

WestBow Press
A Division of Thomas Nelson & Zondervan
1663 Liberty Drive
Bloomington, IN 47403
www.westbowpress.com
1 (866) 928-1240

ISBN: 978-1-9736-2255-0 (sc)
ISBN: 978-1-9736-2257-4 (hc)
ISBN: 978-1-9736-2256-7 (e)

Library of Congress Control Number: 2018903169

Print information available on the last page.

WestBow Press rev. date: 3/27/2018

To Tim Fox,
a true Barnabas in my life,
who encouraged me to write this book

Contents

Introduction

God Wants to Help You Have a Better Life

Would you like to have a better life? If so, I have some good news for you. God wants to help you have a better life. God loves you and desires the best for you. God created our world, and he designed us, so he knows how life works best. He gave us a book in the Bible called Proverbs to explain the choices and actions that will lead to a better life. Proverbs is as close as the Bible comes to giving us an owner's manual for life. Proverbs addresses practical issues such as marriage, parenting, friendships, money management, and how to be happy. Proverbs is specifically addressed to young people, because many of the habits we form in life begin when we are young adults.

I wrote this book because as a pastor I see so many people make bad choices in life, choices that bring them unnecessary pain and suffering. Our lives would be better—happier, calmer, richer, more peaceful—if we would only follow God's advice for how to live. In other words, following God's plan for life is not only the *right* way to live; it is also the *best* way to live. God's instructions for life are not arbitrary; they make life work more smoothly because they complement how we were designed.

The book of Proverbs is largely a random collection of over six hundred short sayings. I have collated these sayings into five megathemes that recur throughout the book: wisdom and folly, right and wrong, relationships, heart and word, and money and the future. Within these five megathemes, I have identified twenty-five specific topics addressed in Proverbs. Our plan is to spend a week on each of these topics. So, in twenty-five weeks—175 days—a little less than six months—we will survey God's advice in this book. Change is an ongoing process, but if you will open your life to this teaching and put it into practice, I believe God can begin to change your life in the next 175 days.

I need to make clear one more thing before we begin this adventure. These instructions for life work best within a faith relationship to Jesus Christ. A person of any religion or no religion can benefit from the practical advice in Proverbs. However, Proverbs is only one part of God's revelation to us in the Bible. The big message of the Bible is that God designed our world and our lives, but we humans have all rebelled against God's design and plan for us. The Bible calls this sin. Our rebellion has fouled up our world, poisoned our relationships, and alienated us from God. The good news of the Bible is that God loves us and is working to save us from our sin and to restore his universe. He has done this first through his revelation to the nation of Israel (recorded in the Old Testament) and ultimately through the revelation of his Son, Jesus (recorded in the New Testament). Jesus came to earth and died on the cross for our sins, taking the consequences of our rebellion, and giving us forgiveness and the promise of eternal life. If we repent of our sin and put our faith in Jesus, we become a new creation. God's plan begins to be restored in our lives. We become a preview of the coming renewal of heaven and earth. Life works best when we know Jesus. So in this book, we will end each week's study of a topic in Proverbs by setting it in the bigger context of the Bible. We will link the teaching of Proverbs to the work and words of Jesus in the New Testament.

If you think your life is perfect the way it is, you are probably not interested in this book. But if you are frustrated with life, or if your life seems out of whack, perhaps you are ready to consider a different approach. Perhaps you are willing to consider God's design for your life. I invite you to join me on this 175-day discovery!

Megatheme 1:
Wisdom and Folly

Proverbs is part of a collection of books in the Bible called wisdom literature (Job, Psalms, Proverbs, Ecclesiastes, and Song of Songs). The biggest megatheme in Proverbs is wisdom. What does it mean to be wise? How does wisdom differ from knowledge? What are the benefits of wisdom? How does one become wise? We will spend the first five weeks of our study on the most important theme in Proverbs.

What Is the Key to a Better Life?

The proverbs of Solomon son of David, king of Israel:
for gaining wisdom and instruction;
for understanding words of insight.
—Proverbs 1:1–2

Proverbs says the key to a better life is to live wisely. This is the theme of the whole book.

Proverbs contains thirty-one chapters. Chapters 10–31 contain more than six hundred one-verse sayings that apply wisdom to different areas of life. Chapters 1–9 do not contain individual proverbs. Instead, these chapters describe the value of wisdom and the keys to becoming wise. Here is a verse that sums up these first nine chapters of Proverbs:

Wisdom is supreme; therefore get wisdom.
Though it costs all you have, get understanding. (Proverbs 4:7)

Most of the proverbs contain two lines each. The second line parallels the first line in some way. The most common parallel is to restate the first line with different wording. That is the pattern in Proverbs 4:7. *Understanding* is a synonym for *wisdom*. Because wisdom is supreme, it is worth any sacrifice to acquire it. You are probably a little skeptical that wisdom is more valuable than all of your possessions. You are probably not yet ready to sacrifice your car or house to get wisdom. That's understandable. For now, at least give wisdom a fair consideration. Then make your own evaluation.

Each day I will suggest a prayer you can pray based upon what we have learned. Here is a suggestion for an opening prayer:

God, I want a better life. I am willing to consider what you have
to say about wisdom in Proverbs. Help me to stick with this study
for the next 175 days. Amen.

What Would a Better Life Look Like?

You will be more motivated to pursue wisdom when you understand its benefits. What does wisdom promise? If you follow the advice God gives in the book of Proverbs, you have the best possible chance for happiness, peace, riches, and long life:

> She is more precious than rubies;
> nothing you desire can compare with her.
> Long life is in her right hand;
> in her left hand are riches and honor.
> Her ways are pleasant ways,
> and all her paths are peace.
> She is a tree of life to those who take hold of her;
> those who hold her fast will be blessed. (Proverbs 3:15–18)

The life of wisdom will also protect you from trouble:

> Then you will go on your way in safety,
> and your foot will not stumble.
> When you lie down, you will not be afraid;
> when you lie down, your sleep will be sweet. (Proverbs 3:23–24)

Would you like to know how to be happy? Would you like to know how you can live at peace? Would you like to know the secret to riches and a long life? Would you like to know how to get rid of your fears and anxieties and get a good night's sleep? That is the better life that wisdom offers!

> God, thank you for revealing in your Word the principles that make life work best. Teach me over the next 174 days the way of life that will lead me to happiness, peace, riches, and long life. Amen.

Choose Wisdom as Early in Life as Possible

My son, do not forget my teaching,
but keep my commands in your heart,
for they will prolong your life many years
and bring you peace and prosperity.
—Proverbs 3:1–2

Proverbs is written to young men. It contains advice from fathers to sons in their teens or twenties. Each of the first seven chapters of Proverbs begins with the address, "My son(s)." This phrase is repeated nineteen times in these seven chapters. There is a masculine quality to Proverbs. However, the wisdom of Proverbs is equally applicable to young women. Some of the images and commands will need to be reversed to apply to girls. For example, Proverbs 6:24 warns young men to beware "the smooth talk of a wayward woman." Young women should be admonished to beware "the smooth talk of a wayward man."

The best time to choose the path of wisdom is when you are young. That is when you are forming many of the habits that will stay with you for the rest of your life. A sign on a rutted road in Alaska read, "Choose your ruts carefully. You will be in them the next fifty miles." If you are in your teens or twenties, this is a critical time in your life. You are choosing patterns of behavior that may set the course of your life for years to come.

If you are now past your twenties, you can't turn back the clock, but you can begin where you are. The sooner you choose the life of wisdom, the more likely you are to reap the benefits of her company.

Dear God, help me to make a fresh start in my life. Help me to choose patterns of behavior that will bless me for years to come. Amen.

Wisdom Must Be Pursued

Blessed are those who find wisdom,
those who gain understanding,
for she is more profitable than silver
and yields better returns than gold.
She is more precious than rubies;
nothing you desire can compare with her.
—Proverbs 3:13–15

Wisdom will not fall into your lap. You must seek wisdom. You must actively pursue wisdom. In Proverbs, wisdom is personified as a woman. Hey, if you are writing a book for young men, doesn't it make sense to portray your lead character as an attractive female? A young man will go to great lengths to impress a prospective girlfriend. Pursue wisdom with the same enthusiasm as a young man pursues the affection of a young woman.

Why should you pursue a life of wisdom with such intensity? Because nothing you desire can compare with the value of wisdom! In 1849, gold was discovered in California. Thousands rushed to California at the prospect of finding the precious metal. In 1848, the population of California was one thousand; by the end of 1849, it had swelled to one hundred thousand! Prospectors sold all they owned and left family and friends to passionately pursue something perceived to have great value. Proverbs says wisdom yields better returns than gold and is worth even greater pursuit. What are you pursuing in life with great passion? Consider directing some of that passion to the pursuit of wisdom. Blessed are those who rush for wisdom.

Dear God, teach me how to be passionate about the pursuit of wisdom in my life. Amen.

Why the Wise Life Works

By wisdom the LORD laid the earth's foundations,
by understanding he set the heavens in place.
—Proverbs 3:19

God can give us a better life because he created us and designed our world. He instilled the principles of wisdom in the very fabric of life on Earth. Reading Proverbs is like reading the instruction book for life. A few years ago, my wife and I purchased a new car. It has all kinds of electronic gadgets that our thirteen-year-old trade-in did not have—navigation system, voice commands, and seat positions that set automatically for different drivers. I did not notice until I left the dealership that the owner's manual was not in the car. I called the dealer, and he promised to mail the owner's manual to us since we lived some distance away. We had to wait a couple of days before it arrived. In the meantime, my wife and I figured out some of the gadgets on our own. Some of them seemed to work intuitively. However, we could not figure out the operation of some features. When the manual arrived, we looked up those features and read the instructions. We had several "aha" moments when we understood the process to get things to work. Many of us are like that in life. We have figured out some things on our own, but we really need the help of an expert—the one who designed life. That is what Proverbs is. It is instruction from the one who designed your life.

> Dear God, I acknowledge that you designed life and that you know how it should work. I am willing to learn what the owner's manual says about how to live life wisely. Amen.

Here's the Fine Print

The teaching of Proverbs on the better life can be misunderstood, so let me add two clarifications. First, I want to be clear that the proverbs are not unconditional guarantees. While there *are* unconditional promises from God in the Bible, that is *not* the nature of the book of Proverbs. These proverbs are general principles of wisdom for life in our world. For example, we have learned that wisdom holds long life in her right hand (Proverbs 3:16). This does not mean that a person who makes wise choices is guaranteed to live a long time. It means that a person who makes wise choices has a much better chance of living a long life. The reason the proverbs are not guarantees is because our world is corrupted by evil. The principles of Proverbs will give you the best chance at a long life, but a wise person can be shot by a gunman. Wise people can get cancer. Wise people can be on a plane that is targeted by terrorists. The principles of Proverbs would work perfectly in Eden, but we do not live in Eden. We certainly cannot say that people who do not live to an old age or who do not get rich are not wise. The circumstances of an evil world may prevent you from living a long life or being healthy or being prosperous, but the life of wisdom will give you the best opportunity to experience a good life in our fallen world.

> Lord Jesus, I know that we live in a fallen world. I pray that you will deliver me from evil. I pray that when I experience the fallout from evil you will help me to cling to your will and your ways. Help me remember what you said, "In this world you will have trouble. But take heart! I have overcome the world" (John 16:33). Amen.

God May Call You to Forfeit the Benefits of Wisdom

There is a second clarification about the benefits of wisdom that I need to share. The wise person may be called by God to forfeit some of the blessings of wisdom for the higher calling of following Christ. The life of wisdom gives me the best chance of experiencing long life, but Christ may call me to lay down my life for him. I must love him more than life. The life of wisdom gives me the best chance of acquiring wealth, but Christ may call me to sell all I have and give to the poor, as he did one young man (Luke 18:18–22). At the same time I am following wise principles, I must listen for the call of God to radical discipleship. Even when we are called to forfeit the benefits of wisdom, the life of wisdom is still the most rewarding life:

> "Truly I tell you," Jesus replied, "no one who has left home or brothers or sisters or mother or father or children or fields for me and the gospel will fail to receive a hundred times as much in this present age: homes, brothers, sisters, mothers, children and fields—along with persecutions—and in the age to come eternal life. (Mark 10:29–30)

In fact, the principles of wisdom in Proverbs will put you in the best position to respond to God's call. When you are physically healthy, financially stable, and emotionally whole, you are best positioned to respond to God's call to missions or ministry.

> Lord, I choose to follow the path that you say will lead to riches, peace, and long life. At the same time, Lord, I am willing to give up riches or peace or long life to be obedient to your call on my life. Help me never let these benefits of wisdom become an idol in my life. May I be willing to lay down anything I possess in order to follow you. Amen.

Be Humble and Teachable

Do not be wise in your own eyes;
fear the Lord and shun evil.
—Proverbs 3:7

What does it mean to live a wise life? How do I get my life headed toward the blessings of wisdom? This proverb summarizes the wise life. The three commands in this verse are the three components of wisdom that we will consider this week. The first component of wisdom is this: don't be wise in your own eyes. The first roadblock to a life of wisdom is to be a know-it-all. To put it another way, pride will prevent you from gaining wisdom. In his book *Failing Forward*, John Maxwell tells the story of John Holiday, the founder and editor of the *Indianapolis News*. One day he stormed out of his office to find the person who had spelled *height* as *hight* in the paper. When someone checked the original copy, it was discovered that Holiday himself was the source of the spelling. He responded, "Well, if that's the way I spelled it, that has to be right." The paper misspelled the word his way for the next thirty years.[1] That's the opposite of a teachable spirit. The first step to wisdom is to recognize you are not wise. We want to appear we have it all together in life. We don't want anyone to see the cracks in our armor. The first step to becoming wise is to recognize your need. The first component of wisdom is to be humble and teachable.

Lord, forgive me when I act like a know-it-all. I confess my pride and ask your forgiveness. I humble myself before you. I want to be teachable in my life. I want to learn the way of wisdom. Thank you for loving and forgiving me. Amen.

To Be Humble and Teachable, Learn to Listen

Have you ever been in a meeting or a class with a person who wanted to talk all the time and impress everyone with what he knew? Do you know someone who thinks he is an expert on any subject that is discussed? Such a person is not likely to be wise. Twelve times in the first nine chapters of Proverbs we are admonished to listen. Here are three examples:

> Let the wise listen and add to their learning,
> and let the discerning get guidance. (Proverbs 1:5)

> Listen, my son, to your father's instruction
> and do not forsake your mother's teaching. (Proverbs 1:8)

> My son, pay attention to my wisdom,
> turn your ear to my words of insight. (Proverbs 5:1)

The emphasis is especially on listening to the advice of parents. When you are young, you tend to think you know more than your parents about life. They dress like dorks and don't listen to the right music, so how could they know how to live? Often it is only in retrospect that you recognize the wisdom of parental advice. Eventually you come to realize that wisdom is not necessarily linked to being an expert on pop culture.

Perhaps someone is trying to give you wise advice, but you refuse to listen. You always have an excuse or a comeback. If you want to have a better life, swallow your pride, shut your mouth, and listen to wise counsel.

> Lord, forgive me for thinking I know more than my parents or for
> disrespecting the wisdom of their generation. Bring wise people
> into my life, and help me to listen to them. Help me to recognize
> your voice through the wise counsel around me. Thank you, Lord,
> for speaking to me through wise people. Amen.

Fear the Lord

Do not be wise in your own eyes;
fear the LORD and shun evil.
This will bring health to your body
and nourishment to your bones.
—Proverbs 3:7–8

The second component of wisdom is to fear the Lord. Our foundational response to God should be that we fear him. This key statement is repeated fifteen times in Proverbs. It means to fear his judgment and respect his authority.

This concept of fearing the Lord is confusing to some people. Can you fear God and love him at the same time? Yes. The Bible says, "Love the Lord your God with all your heart and with all your soul and with all your strength" (Deuteronomy 6:5). The same passage says, "Fear the Lord your God, serve him only" (Deuteronomy 6:13). God is love, and so we love him. God is holy, and so we fear him. Those who have had good parents understand how both these responses are appropriate. I had a good dad. I loved him, but I feared his wrath if I disobeyed him. This balance is described in Acts 9:31, where it says the church was "living in the fear of the Lord and encouraged by the Holy Spirit."

Our culture has lost the concept of fearing the Lord because we have lost a sense of God's holiness. We have a tamed and domesticated concept of God. We do not consider that we should tremble before the Lord Almighty.

Lord, forgive me when I have failed to treat you with respect.
I acknowledge that you are holy. You are completely pure and
righteous. Your greatness and power are beyond my comprehension.
I bow before you as Almighty God. Amen.

What It Means to Fear the Lord

The verses before and after Proverbs 3:7–8 help us understand what it means to fear the Lord. They use three other words to describe a God-centered life.

To fear the Lord is to trust him:

> Trust in the LORD with all your heart
> and lean not on your own understanding. (Proverbs 3:5).

Because God is holy, he is completely dependable and worthy of our trust. We have no reservation about relying on him.

To fear the Lord is to submit to him:

> In all your ways submit to him,
> and he will make your paths straight. (Proverbs 3:6)

Some of us think of God as our servant. His job is to rescue us from problems when we call him, then return to heaven or somewhere until we need him again. A fear of the Lord teaches us to submit to him as our Lord. The benefit is that he will lead us on straight paths.

To fear the Lord is to honor him:

> Honor the LORD with your wealth,
> with the firstfruits of all your crops;
> then your barns will be filled to overflowing,
> and your vats will brim over with new wine. (Proverbs 3:9–10)

These verses refer to giving the first part of your income to the Lord on a regular basis. How do I know if I am honoring God with my life? My giving statement is a tangible indicator of whether I am honoring God. Trust, submission, and honor are all components of what it means to fear the Lord.

> Almighty God, I want to center my life on you. I want to trust
> you, submit to you, and honor you with my life. Amen.

Avoid Evil

Do not be wise in your own eyes;
fear the LORD and shun evil.
This will bring health to your body
and nourishment to your bones.
—Proverbs 3:7–8

The third component of wisdom is to shun evil. Wisdom involves character, integrity, and morality. Wisdom is not just being smart or being an expert in a field. You can be an uneducated person and still be very wise. You can have graduate degrees or be a college professor and still lack wisdom. Wisdom has a moral component. The person who does not shun evil is not wise, regardless of his intelligence.

If you want a better life, shun evil. Many people think the right way to live is not the most fun way to live. They think you trade in happiness for the right life. Proverbs says the right life is also the best life. The devil can give you momentary pleasure, but he cannot sustain it. He can deliver immediate excitement but not long-term happiness. God designed life. His moral commands will bring you the greatest long-term joy in life:

Do not envy the violent
or choose any of their ways.
For the LORD detests the perverse
but takes the upright into his confidence.
The LORD's curse is on the house of the wicked,
but he blesses the home of the righteous. (Proverbs 3:31–33)

I don't want the Lord's curse on my house, do you? I want to shun evil so he can bless my home.

Lord, I recognize that moral compromise will deprive me of the
life of blessing you want for me. I confess my sins of immorality,
dishonesty, deceit, and thievery. I ask your forgiveness. I turn
from these actions. Help me to shun them in the future. Thank
you, Lord. Amen.

The Three Components of Wisdom Cannot Be Separated

> Do not be wise in your own eyes;
> fear the LORD and shun evil.
> This will bring health to your body
> and nourishment to your bones.
> —Proverbs 3:7–8

The order of the phrases in these verses is significant. The fear of the Lord is based upon humility. Shunning evil follows fearing the Lord. These phrases are like layers in a cake; the top layer rests on the layers below it. Some parents grew up fearing the Lord and shunning evil. They no longer fear the Lord, but they still want their children to shun evil. They are trying to have the top layer of the cake without the foundation of the underlying layers. They do not go to church or read the Bible in their home, but they want their kids to have good character. They are puzzled when their children do not share their values. They do not realize those values came from the foundation of fearing the Lord.

We are trying to do the same thing in our nation. We want to teach values in public life, but we want to eliminate any mention of the fear of the Lord lest we offend someone. We cannot build a society of values without a theological foundation for those values. A secular state has no power to produce people of character.

The three components of wisdom are stated together again in Proverbs 8:12–13:

> I, wisdom, dwell together with prudence;
> I possess knowledge and discretion.
> To fear the Lord is to hate evil;
> I hate pride and arrogance;
> evil behavior and perverse speech.

The interconnectedness of these three components is expressed in even stronger terms here. "To fear the Lord is to hate evil." Wisdom "hates pride and arrogance." You won't shun evil until you fear the Lord. You won't fear the Lord unless you are humble.

> Lord, forgive me if I have tried to develop character without being humble and without fearing you. Help me in my home to honor you and teach my children to fear you. Help our nation to recover a fear of the Lord that we may be a people of strong character once again. Amen.

The Life of Wisdom Is Found in Jesus

Jesus emphasized these three components of wisdom in his teaching. Jesus stressed the need to be humble and teachable. Once he called a little child and had him stand among the crowd. He said, "Truly I tell you, unless you change and become like little children, you will never enter the kingdom of heaven. Therefore, whoever takes the lowly position of this child is the greatest in the kingdom of heaven" (Matthew 18:3–4).

Jesus emphasized the need to fear God. Jesus said, "I tell you, my friends, do not be afraid of those who kill the body and after that can do no more. But I will show you whom you should fear: Fear him who, after your body has been killed, has authority to throw you into hell. Yes, I tell you, fear him" (Luke 12:4–5).

Jesus emphasized the moral dimension of wisdom, the need to shun evil. His greatest teaching on this subject is found in the Sermon on the Mount in Matthews 5–7.

> He said, "You have heard that it was said, 'You shall not commit adultery.' But I tell you that anyone who looks at a woman lustfully has already committed adultery with her in his heart. If your right eye causes you to stumble, gouge it out and throw it away. It is better for you to lose one part of your body than for your whole body to be thrown into hell." (Matthew 5:27–29)

The key to a life of wisdom is to listen to the teachings of Jesus and put them into practice: "Therefore everyone who hears these words of mine and puts them into practice is like a wise man who built his house on the rock. The rain came down, the streams rose, and the winds blew and beat against that house; yet it did not fall, because it had its foundation on the rock" (Matthew 7:24–25).

> Lord Jesus, I want my life to be built on solid rock. I want to have the stability to withstand the storms of life. Help me to listen to your words and put them into practice. Amen.

Are You a Fool?

The key to a better life is wisdom. Sometimes we can understand what something is by studying its opposite. The opposite of wisdom, according to Proverbs, is folly. A wise person is one who is teachable, who fears the Lord, and who shuns evil. A fool is a person who does just the opposite. A fool is a person who is not teachable, does not fear the Lord, and does not shun evil. Are you a fool? That's a tough question but is one we need to consider. Being a fool is not a matter of intelligence, education, or station in life. You can be smart and still be a fool. You can be educated and still be a fool. You can be successful and still be a fool. Folly is a spiritual issue and a moral issue.

Proverbs uses five words to describe people who are foolish. These five words reflect three levels of folly, each depicting a state worse than the one before:

The simple
> The stubborn fool
>> The closed-minded fool
>>> The hardened fool
>>>> The mocker

We will spend a day examining what Proverbs has to say about each of these people. As we study these categories, ask yourself, "Do any of these descriptions fit me?"

> Lord, I don't want to be a fool. If there is any level of folly in my
> life, reveal it to me this week. Thank you, Lord. Amen.

The First Prelude to Folly: The Simple Person

The word "simple" (Hebrew: *pethi*) is found fifteen times in Proverbs. It is also translated "naïve" (NASB) or "gullible" (MSG). This is a person who is easily persuaded. The simple person believes anything:

> The simple believe anything,
> but the prudent give thought to their steps. (Proverbs 14:15)

The simple person tends to follow the lead of the people around him. He doesn't think much about where he is going. He lives only for the moment. The simple person is oblivious to spiritual danger. The opposite of a simple person is the prudent person:

> The prudent see danger and take refuge,
> but the simple keep going and pay the penalty. (Proverbs 22:3)

The simple person does not see the seriousness of his choices. This person has not yet made a commitment to the life of wisdom. He is not yet a fool, but he is headed in that direction unless he makes some conscious decisions:

> The simple inherit folly,
> but the prudent are crowned with knowledge. (Proverbs 14:18).

Proverbs is written to youth. Many teenagers are simple. They are easily persuaded; they don't think about where they are going, and they are oblivious to spiritual danger. If that sounds like you, you need to begin to make conscious choices to embrace the components of wisdom. Without those conscious choices, the natural drift of a simple person is toward folly.

> Lord, reveal to me the spiritual naiveté in my life. Show me areas where I am oblivious to spiritual danger. Awaken me to the spiritual battle in my life. Help me choose the life of wisdom. Thank you, Lord, for helping me. Amen.

The Stubborn Fool

The second level of folly is the actual word *fool*. There are three different Hebrew words translated *fool* in Proverbs. We distinguish these three subcategories because they denote a downward slide. The Hebrew word *kesil* is the most common word translated *fool* in Proverbs. It is used about fifty times. It is the mildest form of folly. It refers to someone who is stubborn and obstinate. The gullible, aimless simpleton becomes the stubborn fool. This person begins to look for mischief. He soon finds pleasure in wrongdoing:

> A fool (kesil) finds pleasure in wicked schemes,
> but a person of understanding delights in wisdom. (Proverbs 10:23)

The stubborn fool can be recognized by three characteristics. First, he is hot-headed:

> The wise fear the LORD and shun evil,
> but a fool (kesil) is hotheaded and yet feels secure. (Proverbs 14:16)

Second, the stubborn fool talks too much:

> Fools (kesil) find no pleasure in understanding
> but delight in airing their own opinions. (Proverbs 18:2)

Third, the stubborn fool does not learn from his mistakes:

> As a dog returns to its vomit,
> so fools (kesil) repeat their folly. (Proverbs 26:11)

Instead, the fool begins to blame God for the problems he creates:

> A person's own folly leads to their ruin,
> yet their heart rages against the LORD. (Proverbs 19:3)

> Lord, I confess my stubbornness. I recognize it gets me into trouble. I don't want to continue on this path. Help me, Lord, to be responsive to your will. Amen.

The Close-Minded Fool

The second of three words translated *fool* in Proverbs is the Hebrew word *ewil*. This word is used nineteen times. This person has all the characteristics of a stubborn fool (kesil), but he is even more close-minded. He always thinks he is right:

> The way of fools (ewil) seems right to them,
> but the wise listen to advice. (Proverbs 12:15)

The closed-minded fool will not accept correction:

> A fool (ewil) spurns a parent's discipline,
> but whoever heeds correction shows prudence. (Proverbs 15:5)

The folly of the close-minded fool has become ingrained:

> Though you grind a fool (ewil) in a mortar,
> grinding them like grain with a pestle,
> you will not remove their folly from them. (Proverbs 27:22)

Do you see the downward slide in these descriptions of folly? The aimless, simple person becomes the stubborn fool (kesil) who talks too much and refuses to learn from his mistakes. The stubborn fool soon becomes the close-minded fool (ewil) who always thinks he is right and will not listen to his parents or other sources of wisdom. Do you see any of this pattern in your life?

> Lord, I confess the times I have spurned my parents' discipline and
> rejected your correction in my life. Save me from my folly before
> it becomes ingrained in my life. Thank you for your patience,
> Lord. Amen.

The Hardened Fool

The third word translated *fool* in Proverbs is *nabal*. This word is found only three times in Proverbs. This is the person who has become completely hardened and insensitive to God. A hardened fool brings grief to his parents:

> To have a fool (nabal) for a child brings grief;
> there is no joy for the parent of a godless fool (nabal). (Proverbs 17:21)

We get the clearest picture of this person from another place in scripture, 1 Samuel 25. There was a man named Nabal. David asked Nabal for supplies in exchange for guarding his herds. Nabal refused. Nabal's servants tried to show him his folly, but he would not listen. They told his wife, Abigail, "No one can talk to him" (1 Samuel 25:17). Abigail sent supplies to David and apologized for her husband saying, "Please pay no attention, my lord, to that wicked man Nabal. He is just like his name—his name means Fool, and folly goes with him" (1 Samuel 25:25). The hardened fool denies the very existence of God: "The fool (nabal) says in his heart, 'There is no God'" (Psalm 14:1).

It is a dangerous process to repeatedly reject wise counsel in your life. Repeated rejection hardens your heart. Clay on a potter's wheel can be molded and shaped at will, but after it is hardened, it cannot be reshaped. It can only be broken. Concrete can be manipulated into all kinds of forms, but there is an urgency to working with concrete. There is a limited window of time in which it can be shaped. Once it has hardened, the window of opportunity is closed.

> Lord, I do not want my heart to become hardened. I want to be sensitive to your direction in my life. Change my heart, O Lord. Amen.

The Worst Kind of Folly: the Mocker

Proverbs says that one state is worse than being a fool. The lowest state of folly is to be a mocker. This word *luts* is used seventeen times in Proverbs. The word is also translated *scorner* (KJV) or *scoffer* (NKJV, ESV). This person not only resists wisdom but actively mocks it. The mocker not only refuses correction; he lashes out at it:

> Whoever corrects a mocker invites insults;
> whoever rebukes the wicked incurs abuse.
> Do not rebuke mockers or they will hate you;
> rebuke the wise and they will love you. (Proverbs 9:7–8)

Read the comments following almost any article on the internet, and you will find a string of insults and abusive language. We are becoming a culture of mockers. Christians must not be swept up in this tide of personal attacks. We must learn to disagree with opinions without resorting to verbal abuse and name-calling.

Another characteristic of the mocker is that he incites trouble and division:

> Mockers stir up a city,
> but the wise turn away anger. (Proverbs 29:8)

Mockers use controversial issues as an opportunity to stir up anger, division, and violence. The wise confront issues with peaceful courage.

Mockers go beyond insulting other people. Mockers ultimately mock God. There is a new atheism in our culture that is aggressive and confrontational. Books like *God Is Not Great: How Religion Poisons Everything*, by Christopher Hitchens, and *The God Delusion*, by Richard Hawkins, reflect the fruit of a culture that mocks God.

> Lord, I do not wish to become a person who mocks you. If I am
> headed in that direction, wake me up and turn me around. Thank
> you for your mercy to me. Amen.

Three Levels of Folly: The Simple, Fools, and Mockers

> How long will you who are simple love your simple ways?
> How long will mockers delight in mockery
> and fools hate knowledge?
> —Proverbs 1:22

All three categories of folly—the simple, fools, and mockers—are mentioned in this proverb. You may recognize people you know in these descriptions of folly. More importantly, do you see yourself here? Are you on this downward slide? Is your heart hardening? This is why it is so important to teach children the way of wisdom. The longer we go down the path of folly, the more deeply it becomes ingrained. There is a hardening of the will and the heart that takes place as we refuse, then despise, and then attack wisdom.

I want to end with good news. God can save the simple. He can change the fool:

> For the waywardness of the simple will kill them,
> and the complacency of fools will destroy them;
> but whoever listens to me will live in safety
> and be at ease, without fear of harm. (Proverbs 1:32–33)

This process of transformation takes places by the grace of God, through the rebirth of the Holy Spirit, when we believe in Jesus Christ:

> At one time we too were foolish, disobedient, deceived and enslaved by all kinds of passions and pleasures. We lived in malice and envy, being hated and hating one another. But when the kindness and love of God our Savior appeared, he saved us, not because of righteous things we had done, but because of his mercy. He saved us by the washing of rebirth and renewal by the Holy Spirit, whom he poured out on us generously through Jesus Christ our Savior. (Titus 3:3–6)

> Lord, thank you for your power to change even fools. Thank you for your steadfast love that continues to pursue me. Whatever folly I have discovered in my life this week, I ask you to forgive me and set me on a course to wisdom. Amen.

Beware of Danger

The chapters on wisdom in Proverbs spend a lot of time talking about sexual sin. All of chapter 5, half of chapter 6, and all of chapter 7 warn about the danger of adultery. You might not think of this subject as an integral part of the wise life, but Proverbs says a major temptation that will sidetrack you from a better life is the seduction of adultery:

> My son, pay attention to my wisdom,
> turn your ear to my words of insight.
> that you may maintain discretion
> and your lips may preserve knowledge.
> For the lips of the adulterous woman drip honey,
> and her speech is smoother than oil;
> but in the end she is bitter as gall,
> sharp as a double-edged sword. (Proverbs 5:1–4)

These warnings are written to young men. Young women will need to reverse this imagery. It applies equally to you. The specific subject in Proverbs is adultery with a married woman, but the warnings apply equally to singles concerning premarital sexual activity.

There is a powerful attraction to the sin of adultery, but Proverbs warns that it ends bitterly and brings great pain. It does not produce the good life it promises. This week ask yourself this hard question: Is there a relationship in my life in which I am in danger of inappropriate behavior with the opposite sex?

> Lord, help me this week to evaluate my relationships with the opposite sex. If I am in danger of committing sin, help me to see that danger with clarity of vision. Amen.

Adultery Robs You of the Life God Wants You to Have

Proverbs warns about the detrimental effects of adultery on your life. Adultery—contrary to its promises—robs you of joy and the life God wants you to have.

First, adultery robs you of meaningful relationships and often results in you being alone. Adulterous relationships are usually dead-end relationships. You give your best years away:

> Lest you give your best strength to others
> and your years to one who is cruel. (Proverbs 5:9 NIV, 1984)

Second, adultery robs you of wealth:

> Lest strangers feast on your wealth
> and your toil enrich the house of another. (Proverbs 5:10)

Adultery is a great destroyer of family wealth in our culture. Adultery leads to divorce, lawyer fees, court costs, duplicate households, child support payments, and alimony.

Third, adultery robs you of physical health:

> At the end of your life you will groan,
> when your flesh and body are spent. (Proverbs 5:11)

Even beyond the possibility of disease is the physical stress that ages you.

Fourth, adultery invites a beating from the husband of the unfaithful wife:

> But a man who commits adultery has no sense,
> whoever does so destroys himself.
> Blows and disgrace are his lot,
> and his shame will never be wiped away. (Proverbs 6:32–33)

> Lord, when I am tempted to commit sexual sin, remind me of the consequences of this sin in my life. Amen.

Adultery Ultimately Leads to Death

The worst effect of adultery is that it leads to death:

> Her feet go down to death;
> her steps lead straight to the grave. (Proverbs 5:5)

Proverbs 7 illustrates this verse. The entire chapter is a narrative of a simple man who is seduced by an adulteress. She flirts with him and kisses him and tells him her husband is out of town on business. She tells him that her bed is perfumed with myrrh, aloe, and cinnamon. Proverbs warns that he is being ensnared like an animal:

> With persuasive words she led him astray;
> she seduced him with her smooth talk.
> All at once he followed her
> like an ox going to the slaughter,
> like a deer stepping into a noose
> till an arrow pierces its liver,
> like a bird darting into a snare,
> little knowing it will cost him his life.
> Now then, my sons, listen to me;
> pay attention to what I say.
> Do not let your heart turn to her ways
> or stray into her paths.
> Many are the victims she has brought down;
> her slain are a mighty throng.
> Her house is a highway to the grave,
> leading down to the chambers of death.(Proverbs 7:21–27)

The death that Proverbs warns about may be physical death. Proverbs tells you how to have a long life through wisdom. Adultery can cut short your life. The death described may also be spiritual death. Unless there is repentance, the road of adultery leads to hell. The New King James Version translates verse 27: "Her house is the way to hell." In the game of adultery, the stakes are very high.

> Lord, open my eyes to the high stakes involved in sexual sin, that
> I may avoid the road to death. Amen.

Steer Clear of the Adulterous Person

How can one avoid the seduction and pain of adultery? Proverbs offers three strategies. The first strategy is to stay away from this type of person:

> Keep to a path far from her,
> do not go near the door of her house. (Proverbs 5:8)

You cannot run from all sexual temptation. This is not the ultimate solution. But there are some types of people of the opposite sex that you need to avoid. They are on the hunt. They are seeking to fill a need or are seeking a conquest. Stay far from them; do not go near them.

The first strategy for avoiding sexual sin is to place some boundaries in your life. There are places in your city you do not need to go. There are places in conversations where you must refuse to go. There are places on the internet where you must refuse to go. If you can identify the place where you are most likely to get into trouble, just don't go there. It's not worth it.

One of the most important places to create boundaries is in the workplace. In her book *Avoiding the Greener Grass Syndrome: How to Grow Affair-Proof Hedges around Your Marriage*, Nancy Anderson shares a list of practical steps to create boundaries in the workplace.[2] These include:

1. Talk about your spouse in positive terms.
2. The only appropriate touch between business associates of the opposite sex is a handshake.
3. Make sure emails and other communications are not suggestive or flirtatious.
4. When on business travel, meet associates of the opposite sex in the lobby rather than in a hotel room.

These boundaries are not the whole strategy for avoiding sexual sin, but they are good first steps.

> Lord, help me be wise in my relationship with the opposite sex. Help me set appropriate boundaries in my life. Help me form relationships with those who value the same things I value. Amen.

Find Satisfaction in Your Own Marriage

The second strategy for avoiding the pain of adultery is to strengthen your marriage and find joy there. Fight a negative temptation with a positive relationship:

> Drink water from your own cistern,
> running water from your own well.
> May your fountain be blessed,
> and may you rejoice in the wife of your youth.
> May you ever be intoxicated with her love. (Proverbs 5:15, 18–19)

Expend the energy on your marriage that you are tempted to expend on impressing and pursuing someone outside your marriage. Instead of becoming intoxicated with the affection of someone at work, become intoxicated with the love of your own wife. Laugh and flirt with your own spouse rather than with someone else.

Focus on the positives in your own marriage. You tend to see your partner in the worst conditions and your tempter in the best circumstances. Look for the good things in your relationship with your spouse and celebrate those good things. Many men tend to be problem-solvers. That causes us to focus on what is wrong and what needs to be changed. This works well when you are dealing with a car: identify the problem and correct the problem. This approach does not work so well in a marriage. It will cause you to be focused on the negatives in your spouse. It will cause you to become frustrated because you cannot "fix" another person. The better approach is to focus on what is good in your marriage. Look for the good. Thank God for the good. Tell your wife that you appreciate the good. This will change your attitude, honor your wife, and result in thanksgiving to God.

> Lord, help me to love my spouse. Help me focus on the good
> things in my marriage. Bring us together and strengthen our
> relationship. Amen.

Embrace a Life of Wisdom

The third strategy for avoiding the pain of adultery is to embrace a life of wisdom. This is the deepest and most important of the three strategies. Get serious about the life of wisdom. Wisdom will protect you from danger:

> My son, keep my words
> and store up my commands within you.
> Keep my commands and you will live;
> guard my teachings as the apple of your eye.
> Bind them on your fingers;
> write them on the tablet of your heart.
> Say to wisdom, "You are my sister,"
> and to insight, "You are my relative."
> They will keep you from the adulterous woman,
> from the wayward woman with her seductive words. (Proverbs 7:1–5)

We have learned that the first component of wisdom is being teachable and listening to good counsel. Many Christians on the path toward adultery have someone in their lives who is warning them about the danger of the relationship, but they do not listen. Allow godly friends to speak truth to you and hold you accountable.

The second component of wisdom is to fear God. A healthy fear of God's wrath is an effective deterrent to adultery. We may hide our sin from everyone else, but we cannot hide it from God. "We must all appear before the judgment seat of Christ, so that each of us may receive what is due us for the things done while in the body, whether good or bad" (2 Corinthians 5:10).

The third component of wisdom is to shun evil. Don't try to see how close you can get to the edge of the cliff without falling off. The way to avoid falling is to stay a healthy distance back from the edge. It is when you play with fire that you get burned.

> Lord, I want to be serious about these three components of wisdom in my life. Help me long for wisdom more than I lust for anything else. Amen.

What If I Have Already Committed Adultery?

Proverbs warns young people to avoid the pain of adultery. It focuses on prevention. What if you have already gone down the road of promiscuity or adultery? Is there any hope for you? Yes, you can be forgiven of your sin and have a fresh start in life. Jesus once talked with a woman who had been caught in the act of adultery. He said to her, "Go now and leave your life of sin" (John 8:11). Forgiveness does not erase the consequences of your action, but forgiveness brings you into right standing with God and releases you from guilt. You can be washed, sanctified, and justified in the name of Jesus (1 Corinthians 6:9–11).

So, if you want to make a new start, you need to do three things. First, get down on your knees and ask God to forgive your sin. Call upon the name of Jesus. Ask him to change your heart. He will cleanse you! Commit yourself to the life of wisdom.

Second, call the person with whom you have had an affair and explain that the relationship is over. Confess that you have sinned. Explain that you will never call or see him or her again (unless there is a child from the relationship, which will necessitate a modified relationship).

Third, confess your sin to your spouse and ask his or her forgiveness. There is no guarantee your spouse will be open to reconciliation, but this is the step you must take. If your spouse is willing to forgive and reconcile, it will take time to rebuild trust. You and your spouse may need a Christian counselor to help you work through problems of anger, guilt, and trust.

If you are a Christian single who has been involved in promiscuity, confess your sin to God and accept his offer of forgiveness. End the relationship immediately. Take a pledge of purity from this time forward.

> Jesus, I confess my sin to you. I ask your forgiveness. I ask you to wash me, cleanse me, and remove my guilt. I ask you to transform me and make me a different person. I ask you to help me as I deal with the consequences of my sin. Thank you, Jesus. Amen.

A Woman Named Wisdom Is Calling You

Proverbs 8–9 is a summary and conclusion of the first nine chapters of the book. These two chapters contain a personification of wisdom. Personification is a literary device in which qualities of a person are given to something that is not personal. We use personification when we say, "Opportunity is knocking at your door," or "My computer is grumpy today," or "I hear the beach calling me."

Wisdom is personified as a woman in chapters 8–9. Remember this book is written to young men. Girls might switch the imagery to a guy. This woman named Wisdom is calling to young men. Chapter 7 depicted another woman calling to young men. That chapter was about the seduction of adultery, one of the great threats to a life of wisdom. In contrast to that call, Lady Wisdom is also calling:

> Does not wisdom call out?
> Does not understanding raise her voice?
> At the highest point along the way,
> where the paths meet, she takes her stand. (Proverbs 8:1–2)

Most of us can remember where we were when we heard the news of some major event. Novelist David Lodge tells where he was when he heard of the assassination of President Kennedy in 1963. He was in a theater watching a play, a comedy. In one scene a character turned on a radio. The actor always tuned in to a real broadcast to add realism. Suddenly the announcement came on the radio that the president had been shot. The actor quickly turned off the radio, but it was too late. Reality had interrupted comedy.[3] The voice of wisdom is like that, calling out to us in unexpected ways, interrupting the pretense of our lives to tell us truth.

> God, this passage says your wisdom is calling to me. I don't want
> to miss her voice. Slow me down and calm my heart, so that I can
> hear what you have to say to me. Amen.

Are You Listening?

Beside the gate leading into the city,
at the entrance, she cries aloud:
To you, O people, I call out;
I raise my voice to all mankind.
You who are simple, gain prudence;
you who are foolish, set your hearts on it.
Listen, for I have trustworthy things to say;
I open my lips to speak what is right.
—Proverbs 8:3–6

We often think God is silent. We pray and ask him to give us direction, but we do not think he responds very promptly or clearly. We think he needs to do a better job communicating with us. This passage says God's wisdom is calling out everywhere. She is speaking openly in the cities. She is calling out to all mankind. She seeks to gain the attention of the simple and fools. The problem is not that there is no guidance from God but that we are not listening. We are not aware of his communication. The problem is not with God's transmitter but with our receiver. We are not on the right channel. We are like the guy who complains to his friend, "I want to watch football! There has been nothing on but cooking shows all day!" His friend responds, "Dude, that's because you are on the Food Channel. If you want to watch sports, you might try changing the channel to ESPN." Perhaps you are complaining that you do not hear God, but you are not on his channel. You are tuned in to other networks, and so you are missing the voice of wisdom calling you. God loves you. He is trying to steer you away from bad choices and into a relationship with him. You don't hear him because you refuse to turn to his channel.

Dear God, forgive me for accusing you of being silent. Help me know how to change the channel so I can hear your voice. Amen.

Tune In to Truth

How can we get on God's channel and hear wisdom calling? First, tune in to truth and righteousness:

> My mouth speaks what is true,
> for my lips detest wickedness.
> All the words of my mouth are just;
> none of them is crooked or perverse.
> To the discerning all of them are right;
> they are upright to those who have found knowledge. (Proverbs 8:7–8)

Deceit, deception, and lying are not in the company of wisdom. The mouth of wisdom speaks what is true. Anything crooked or perverse is not wise. If you are preoccupied with cheating or scheming, you will not hear the voice of wisdom. Change the channel. Determine to speak the truth, value the truth, and listen to those who speak truth. Then you will begin to hear the voice of wisdom.

Casting Crowns has a song entitled "The Voice of Truth." The verses of the song describe the various voices that call out lies to us. The chorus responds:

> But the voice of truth tells me a different story
> And the voice of truth says, "Do not be afraid!"
> And the voice of truth says, "This is for my glory."
> Out of all the voices calling out to me
> I will choose to listen and believe the voice of truth.

> Lord, I confess any deceit or lying in my life. I ask your forgiveness.
> I don't want to be on that channel any more. Give me the power
> to speak the truth and love the truth. Thank you, Lord. Amen.

Don't Let Material Things Dominate Your Thoughts

The second key to hearing the voice of wisdom is this: Don't let material things dominate your thoughts and choices.

> Choose my instruction instead of silver,
> knowledge rather than choice gold,
> for wisdom is more precious than rubies,
> and nothing you desire can compare with her. (Proverbs 8:10–11)

The quest for riches can consume a person and detract from the search for wisdom. Martin Luther said, "Even a penny, when held close enough to one's eye, can blot out heaven."

Deliberately choose the pursuit of wisdom over the pursuit of wealth. This is what Solomon did when he became king.

> Now, LORD my God, you have made your servant king in place of my father David. But I am only a little child and do not know how to carry out my duties … So give your servant a discerning heart to govern your people and to distinguish between right and wrong. The Lord was pleased that Solomon had asked for this. So God said to him, "Since you have asked for this and not for long life or wealth for yourself, nor have asked for the death of your enemies but for discernment in ministering justice, I will do what you have asked. I will give you a wise and discerning heart, so that there will never have been anyone like you, nor will there ever be. Moreover, I will give you what you have not asked for—both wealth and honor—so that in your lifetime you will have no equal among kings. (1 Kings 3:7, 9–13)

God was pleased that Solomon focused his desires on wisdom rather than wealth. God gave Solomon both wisdom and wealth. A blind pursuit of money will easily drown out the voice of wisdom.

> Lord, I am too often preoccupied with material things. Today I choose to put my focus on you instead. I do not want my pursuit of money to cause me to miss the voice of wisdom. Amen.

Who Is This Lady Wisdom?

Proverbs 8:22–31 is one of the most debated passages in Proverbs. Lady Wisdom is still talking. She is making the point of how important it is to listen to her. This passage says she has been with God since before creation:

> The LORD brought me forth as the first of his works,
> before his deeds of old;
> I was formed long ages ago,
> at the very beginning, when the world came to be …
> Before the mountains were settled in place,
> before the hills, I was given birth …
> Then I was constantly at his side.
> I was filled with delight day after day,
> rejoicing always in his presence,
> rejoicing in his whole world
> and delighting in mankind. (Proverbs 8:22–23, 25, 30–31)

Throughout church history, Christians have debated whether this passage refers to Jesus. Many early Christian teachers, such as Justin Martyr in AD 125, said that it did. Jesus was certainly present at creation. Could *Wisdom* be a name for Jesus like *Word* in John 1:1? The problem with applying this to Jesus is a phrase in Proverbs 8:22: "I was formed long ago." Though this verse can be translated different ways, it seems to say wisdom was the first of God's creations.

In the fourth century, there was a controversy about the nature of Christ. A teacher named Arius said that Christ had a beginning and that he was not equal with God. Arius pointed to this verse as evidence. At the Council of Nicaea, the teaching of Arius was rejected, and the Nicene Creed was formulated. It asserts that Jesus is coequal with the Father from eternity. Lady Wisdom is not the same as Jesus, but you can see why the comparison is made. In Christ "are hidden all the treasures of wisdom and knowledge" (Colossians 2:3). If you want the benefits of a wise life, come to Jesus. All the treasures of wisdom are hidden in him.

> Jesus, I believe you are the source of all wisdom. I want to know you and follow you. Impart your wisdom to me, I pray. Thank you, Jesus. Amen.

Two Women Are Calling You

This section closes with a final call from Lady Wisdom. She is inviting you to come to her house for a banquet of wonderful food:

> Wisdom has built her house;
> she has set up its seven pillars.
> She has prepared her meat and mixed her wine;
> she has also set her table.
> She has sent out her servants, and she calls
> from the highest point of the city,
> "Let all who are simple come to my house!"
> To those who have no sense she says,
> "Come, eat my food
> and drink the wine I have mixed.
> Leave your simple ways and you will live;
> walk in the ways of insight. (Proverbs 9:1–6)

What a wonderful invitation! Why doesn't everyone accept God's invitation to enjoy the blessings of a wise life? There is a competing voice offering an invitation to a different party. Folly is also personified as a woman calling to you:

> Folly is an unruly woman;
> she is simple and knows nothing.
> She sits at the door of her house,
> on a seat at the highest point of the city,
> calling out to those who pass by,
> who go straight on their way,
> "Let all who are simple come to my house!"
> To those who have no sense she says,
> "Stolen water is sweet;
> food eaten in secret is delicious!"
> But little do they know that the dead are there,
> that her guests are deep in the realm of the dead. (Proverbs 9:13–18)

This woman mimics Wisdom, but she is loud and crass. The menu for her party is only bread and water. She cannot compete with the quality of life Wisdom offers. Her guests die in her home. Two women are wooing you, inviting you to their homes. Which invitation will you accept?

> Lord, give me discernment to choose between the competing voices clamoring for my attention in life. Help me to accept those invitations which will honor you and bless me. Amen.

There Are Only Two Real Options in Life

How will you live? There are only two real options in life. There is the way of wisdom and the way of folly. The world says there are many options concerning how to live. The Bible repeatedly narrows the list of choices to two. Jesus hammered these same two choices home in the conclusion of his Sermon on the Mount. He said we all choose one of two roads in life: "Enter through the narrow gate. For wide is the gate and broad is the road that leads to destruction, and many enter through it. But small is the gate and narrow the road that leads to life, and only a few find it" (Matthew 7:13–14).

Jesus said we bear one of two kinds of fruit: "A good tree cannot bear bad fruit, and a bad tree cannot bear good fruit. Every tree that does not bear good fruit is cut down and cast into the fire. Thus, by their fruits you will recognize them" (Matthew 7:18-20).

Jesus said everyone builds his life on one of two foundations: "Therefore everyone who hears these words of mine and puts them into practice is like a wise man who built his house on the rock … But everyone who hears these words of mine and does not put them into practice is like a foolish man who built his house on sand" (Matthew 7:24, 26). We all start out on the broad road, bearing bad fruit, building on a poor foundation. Unless we make a conscious choice, we inherit folly. The default road is the road that leads to destruction. The good news is that you can take a different road. As you hear the word of God, you are at a crossroad in your life. Wisdom is calling you to turn in her direction. Listen. Do you hear her calling?

> Jesus, I hear the voice of wisdom calling me. I want to get off the road that leads to destruction. I choose your way, Jesus. I want to enter through the small gate and follow the narrow road. I want to bear good fruit. I want my life built upon the rock. Help me, Jesus, as I begin to follow you. Amen.

Megatheme 2:
Righteousness and Wickedness

We now turn our attention primarily to the individual, one-verse proverbs contained in Proverbs 10–29. Related to the choice between wisdom and folly is the choice between righteousness and wickedness. This is the second biggest theme in Proverbs. About one hundred of the six hundred proverbs in Proverbs 10–29 contain the words "righteous" or "wicked." Righteousness means to do what is right, to be honest and truthful, to treat people fairly, and to be obedient to parents and the law. Wickedness is the opposite. It is to be unfair, untruthful, and unlawful. The wise person chooses righteousness over wickedness. We will spend the next five weeks learning how righteousness leads to a better life.

The Right Way and the Wrong Way

The righteous detest the dishonest;
the wicked detest the upright.
—Proverbs 29:27

Is there really such a thing as right and wrong? Our culture is moving toward moral relativism, the belief that there is no absolute right or wrong. Friedrich Nietzsche wrote, "You have your way. I have my way. As for the right way, the correct way, the only way, it does not exist." Ravi Zacharias has pointed out that relativism cannot be true. Relativism says, "All truth is relative." However, either that statement is relative and not dependable, or that statement is an absolute and thus there are absolute truths. C. S. Lewis wrote that we all know innately that there are moral absolutes. He pointed out that when we quarrel we say things like, "That's not fair" or "I was here first."[4] A sense of right and wrong is built into our human nature.

Proverbs is adamant that there is a clear distinction between right and wrong. As with wisdom and folly, Proverbs simplifies life and boils it down to two basic orientations. Proverbs presents a clear choice between the life of wisdom and righteousness on the one hand and the life of folly and wickedness on the other. Our tendency is to blur the distinction between these two ways of life. We think of ourselves as "somewhat righteous" or "not very wicked." Proverbs forces us to examine the basic orientation of our lives. It says these two ways of life are diametrically opposed to one another.

> Lord, help me this week to see clearly the basic orientation of my life. Help me to choose to become a righteous person. Thank you, Lord. Amen.

The Contrast between Righteousness and Wickedness

Of the one hundred or so proverbs that contain the words *righteousness* or *wickedness*, about sixty of them contrast these two ways of life. Each proverb has two lines. These proverbs say "Righteousness is (or does) this, but wickedness is (or does) that." Let's look at some of these contrasts.

The righteous and wicked can be discerned by the company they keep:

> The righteous choose their friends carefully,
> but the way of the wicked leads them astray. (Proverbs 12:26)

The righteous are differentiated from the wicked by their conversation:

> The heart of the righteous weighs its answers,
> but the mouth of the wicked gushes evil. (Proverbs 15:28)

The righteous have a concern for the poor that is lacking in the wicked:

> The righteous care about justice for the poor,
> but the wicked have no such concern. (Proverbs 29:7)

The righteous and the wicked can even be distinguished by their treatment of animals:

> A righteous man cares for the needs of his animal,
> but the kindest acts of the wicked are cruel.
> (Proverbs 12:10)

Thus, righteousness is revealed by the concrete actions of our day-to-day lives. Righteousness is revealed in our circle of friends, our conversations, how we treat the poor, and even how we treat animals.

> Holy Spirit, I need to take inventory of my life today. Reveal to me through these scriptures my true character. Help me to cut through my excuses and see myself as you see me. I confess any sin you reveal to me, and with your help I will seek to change my life. Amen.

Choices Have Consequences

Of the sixty proverbs that contrast righteousness and wickedness, twenty-six of them contrast the outcomes of these two ways of life. You can choose how you will live, but your choices have consequences. Proverbs says the wise way to make choices is to look ahead and see where those choices will lead you:

> Blessings crown the head of the righteous,
> but violence overwhelms the mouth of the wicked. (Proverbs 10:6)

> The prospect of the righteous is joy,
> but the hopes of the wicked come to nothing. (Proverbs 10:28)

> The righteous eat to their hearts' content,
> but the stomach of the wicked goes hungry. (Proverbs 13:25)

> The house of the wicked contains great treasure,
> but the income of the wicked brings ruin. (Proverbs 15:6)

> Truly the righteous attain life,
> but whoever pursues evil finds death. (Proverbs 11:19)

Look at these two lists. Which list do you want for your life? The way to experience the outcome is to make the choice that God says will lead to that outcome. Where is your life taking you?

Righteousness leads to:	Wickedness leads to:
Blessings	Violence
Joy	Disappointment
Contentment	Hunger
Treasure	Ruin
Life	Death

> Lord, help me not to be shortsighted in the choices I make. Give me the vision to look far ahead and visualize where my choices are leading me. Help me make choices that will lead to joy, contentment, treasure, and life. Amen.

41

Direct Your Desires to Good Things

How do you make righteous choices? First, direct your desires toward good things. The unfaithful are trapped by evil desires:

> The righteousness of the upright delivers them,
> but the unfaithful are trapped by evil desires. (Proverbs 11:6)

> The desire of the righteous ends only in good,
> but the hope of the wicked only in wrath. (Proverbs 11:23)

> The wicked desire the stronghold of evildoers,
> but the root of the righteous endures. (Proverbs 12:12)

Here is a tip from driver's education: you tend to steer in the direction you look. So look where you want to go. Don't stare at that oncoming truck to your left or at the steep embankment to your right. Focus on the lane ahead of you.

This advice also applies to life. Direct your eyes toward what is good, and you will begin to desire what is good. What do you set before your eyes every morning? What do you read or watch every night? Do you routinely focus on worthless and trivial things? Do you direct your eyes to the Bible every morning or every evening? Like many people, I tend to check the internet every morning to see what is happening in the world. However, a quick check of the news easily leads to chasing other worthless headlines. Before I know it, I am reading about "Ten Stars of 1970s Sitcoms and What They Look Like Today." Lately I have written the following verse on my computer wallpaper: "Turn my eyes away from worthless things; preserve my life according to your word" (Psalm 119:37). Set your desires on good things and your choices will be wise.

> Lord God, today I choose to set the desires of my heart on that
> which is good and pleasing to you. Amen.

Remember That God Is Watching You

How do you make righteous choices? First, direct your desire toward good things. Second, remember that God is watching you:

> The eyes of the Lord are everywhere,
> keeping watch on the wicked and the good. (Proverbs 15:3)

Surveillance is a powerful deterrent to unrighteousness. When I was a child, I tended to behave better when my parents were watching than when their eyes were not on me. Not long ago I was approaching an intersection, and the traffic light turned yellow. I thought I could "beat the light," but then I noticed a camera mounted near the traffic signal. I decided to put on the brakes. We will be more righteous people when we cultivate an awareness that God is always watching us. He watches in order to evaluate the righteousness of our lives. The books of Kings and Chronicles describe the reigns of the kings of Israel and Judah. At the end of almost every account there is one of two summary statements: "He did what was right in the eyes of the Lord," or "He did what was evil in the eyes of the Lord." What would be the Lord's summary statement about our lives?

The Lord not only sees all we do, but he even knows our thoughts:

> The Lord detests the thoughts of the wicked,
> but gracious words are pure in his sight. (Proverbs 15:26)

Real righteousness is not just a matter of what we do. Real righteousness is a matter of attitude and motivation and desire. Our thoughts lie open before the Lord.

> O Lord, I know that your eyes are upon me. I realize that you
> know my deepest thoughts. Give me an awareness of your presence
> today so that I may not be drawn to evil. Thank you, Lord. Amen.

When You Fall Down, Get Back Up

How do you make righteous choices? First, direct your desires toward good things. Second, remember that God is watching you. Third, when you fall down, get back up:

> For though the righteous fall seven times, they rise again,
> but the wicked stumble when calamity strikes. (Proverbs 24:16)

This is one of my favorite proverbs. No one is perfect. The righteous are not exempt from falling. But the righteous do not stay down. The righteous sometimes make bad choices, but they do not let those individual choices define them. There is a persistence to the righteous. They refuse to be brought down. They keep getting back up!

If you have made a bad choice recently, let me offer you some encouragement. That bad choice does not have to define who you are. Do not let it defeat you. Get up now! Get back on track immediately! When cranberries are harvested, they must pass a "bounce test" that separates firm berries from soft or rotten ones. The cranberries are poured over a series of steps. Only those that bounce over a low barrier pass the quality test. There is a bounce test in your life that will reveal the quality of your character. Will you bounce back from failure?

What if you have made this same mistake over and over? Keep getting back up until your life is defined by standing and not by falling. Author John Creasey received 743 rejection slips from publishers before one word was ever published. He eventually published 560 books, which sold more than sixty million copies. Oscar Hammerstein had five flop shows, which lasted less than a combined total of six week, before *Oklahoma*, which ran for 269 weeks and grossed $7 million.[5] It is not so much how you start that matters. It is how you finish that counts.

> O Lord, I do not want to be defined by my bad choices. I want to get back up. Help me to overcome the discouragement of the devil and make a new beginning. Thank you, Lord. Amen.

Is Anyone Righteous?

In the New Testament, the book of Romans continues the theme of righteousness. It says, "There is no one is righteous, not even one" (Romans 3:10). Wow! That is bad news. We have all made wicked choices. We are all headed for the disappointment and trouble and death described in Proverbs.

Romans also contains good news. It says that if we place our faith in Jesus, God will credit our faith as righteousness (Romans 4:23–24). How can God do that? How can he simply count our faith as righteousness? Jesus paid the penalty for our sin, so that the righteous requirements of the law have been fully met:

> For what the law was powerless to do because it was weakened by the flesh, God did by sending his own Son in the likeness of sinful flesh to be a sin offering. And so he condemned sin in the flesh, in order that the righteous requirement of the law might be fully met in us, who do not live according to the flesh but according to the Spirit. (Romans 8:3–4)

Does that mean that our choices about righteousness no longer matter? No! Because we have been declared righteous, we are motivated to choose righteousness as a way of life: "You have been set free from sin and have become slaves to righteousness … so now offer yourselves as slaves to righteousness leading to holiness" (Romans 6:18–19). We offer ourselves to righteousness in gratitude to the God who freed us from slavery to sin.

> Father, I admit that I am not righteous. Thank you for loving me in spite of my wickedness. Lord Jesus, thank you for taking the punishment for my sin and giving me your righteous standing before God. I place my faith in you. I commit myself to a life of righteousness in gratitude for your salvation. Amen.

Righteousness Involves Honesty

Honest scales and balances belong to the Lord;
all the weights in the bag are of his making.
—Proverbs 16:11

We are learning about the second megatheme in Proverbs: righteousness and wickedness. Now we want to begin to focus on some of the specific choices concerning righteousness or wickedness. The first component of righteousness is honesty. You have a choice between honesty and dishonesty. This proverb tells us that God cares a great deal about honesty.

We would be better off as a society and as individuals if we cared as much as God does about honesty. According to the Uniform Crime Reports, there are over one million cases of shoplifting a year.[6] This costs each US household a "crime tax" of over $400 per year in higher retail costs.[7]

The FBI says insurance fraud costs us $40 billion a year. The average family pays $700 more per year in insurance premiums because of false claims, agents who skim profits, and other scams.[8]

The IRS estimates the tax gap caused by those who cheat on taxes (those who underreport, underpay, or do not file) is over $450 billion per year.[9] This is about 17 percent of annual tax revenue and is almost equal to the budget deficit. Here is my plan to lower taxes: don't cheat! We would be far better off economically if we obeyed God's commands.

Lord, help me to examine my life this week for dishonesty. Break through my rationalizations and my self-deception so that I may see myself as you see me. Amen.

God Desires Honesty in Business

The Lord detests dishonest scales,
but accurate weights find favor with him.
—Proverbs 11:1

In the days when Proverbs was written, a dishonest seller would keep two sets of weights. (Let's use modern standards of measurement to illustrate.) If you wanted to buy a pound of figs, he would pull out a stone labeled "one pound" that was really a little less than a pound. He would place it on his balance scales, and you would receive a little less than a pound of figs. If you wanted to sell a pound of figs, he would pull out a stone labeled "one pound" that was really heavier than a pound. He would place it on his balance scales and get more than a pound of figs.

I am reminded of the story of a woman who stopped at a butcher shop to buy a chicken for dinner. The butcher placed a chicken on the scales behind the counter and told her its weight. She said, "I really need a bit larger chicken." That was his last chicken, so he took it off the scales, rummaged behind the counter, and placed the same chicken back on the scales. "This one weighs a pound more," he announced. The woman thought for a moment and said, "Okay, I'll take them both."

God is a God of truth, and he hates deception in business. God hates manipulation and false representation in business. God delights in accurate gas pumps, accurate scales in the grocery store, and correct change in a sales transaction. God takes pleasure in truthful expense accounts, accurate ledgers, and accurate commissions. God delights when salespeople present products and services accurately. God is interested in and involved in the business of everyday life. Is the business of your life pleasing to God?

> Lord, help me to hate dishonesty just as you hate dishonesty.
> Help me to abhor dishonesty in my own life as much as I hate it
> in others. Bring to my mind right now any lack of integrity in my
> life so that I may turn from it. Amen.

God Is Not Happy with Your Worship If You Are Dishonest

To do what is right and just
is more acceptable to the Lord than sacrifice.
—Proverbs 21:3

This is an incredible statement in its Old Testament context. God is the one who prescribed the Old Testament system of animal sacrifice as the pattern of worship. He designed it as a way for sinful humans to approach a holy God. He expected his people to follow its rules carefully. Yet, God says in this proverb that justice is an even more important form of worship than sacrifice. He implies that he will not accept sacrifices that are offered from a dishonest, unrepentant person.

We often try to separate our lives into compartments. We think we are good Christians because we go to church on Sunday, read our Bibles, and give a tithe to the church. We think this has little to do with how we conduct our business Monday through Friday. We may even think our faithful worship on Sunday "makes up" for some dubious business practices the rest of the week. God will not let us engage in this compartmentalization of our lives. Cecil Day, the founder of the Days Inn motel chain, said that three questions shaped his every business decision: Is it right? Is it fair? Is it true to my Christian commitment?

> Lord, help me to see my work on Monday as much as an act of worship as my church attendance on Sunday. Lord, is there any hypocrisy in my life? I want my workweek to please you. Amen.

God Looks for Honesty in Leaders

Eloquent lips are unsuited to a godless fool—
how much worse lying lips to a ruler!
—Proverbs 17:7

By justice a king gives a country stability,
but those who are greedy for bribes tear it down.
—Proverbs 29:4

It is especially important that leaders in business, government, or church be people of integrity. When such leaders are dishonest, the effect of their sin is multiplied because of their influence. There is greater pressure for leaders to compromise their integrity because some people will benefit from their favoritism or corruption.

Let us pray for our leaders to be people of integrity. Pray for your president, your CEO, your community leaders, and your pastor. Pray that they will resist the temptation to lie or accept bribes or embezzle. Determine that you will not vote for a leader who lacks personal integrity, no matter how impressive his skills or rhetoric. Theodore Roosevelt said:

> No community is healthy where it is ever necessary to distinguish one politician among his fellows because "he is honest." Honesty is not so much a credit as an absolute prerequisite to efficient service to the public. Unless a man is honest we have no right to keep him in public life, it matters not how brilliant his capacity, it hardly matters how great his power of doing good service on certain lines may be.[10]

If you are in a position of leadership, determine ahead of time that you will not compromise your integrity. Ask God to help you see clearly what is right and what is wrong.

> Lord, help me to value integrity in my life and in the lives of others. Give us leaders at every level who are people of honesty and character. Amen.

God Desires Just Legal Systems

An honest witness tells the truth,
but a false witness tells lies.
—Proverbs 12:17

Acquitting the guilty and condemning the innocent—
the Lord detests them both.
—Proverbs 17:15

It is not good to be partial to the wicked
and so deprive the innocent of justice.
—Proverbs 18:5

Do not testify against your neighbor without cause—
would you use your lips to mislead?
—Proverbs 24:28

God desires justice and fairness in our courts. The many proverbs on this subject reflect how important this is to God. God is greatly concerned for the powerless in society. He detests oppression and the abuse of power in a judicial system. If we share God's heart for justice, what can we do? We can renounce two things in our lives that fuel injustice.

First, we can renounce greed in our lives. Greed is the first root of corruption in our legal systems. It causes us to hedge the truth under oath. It causes us to file lawsuits in order to experience a financial windfall. Our society has become obsessed with litigation. In our culture we often see tragedy as an opportunity to benefit financially.

Second, we can renounce prejudice in our lives. Prejudice is the second root of corruption in our legal systems. Prejudice means to prejudge people regarding their innocence or guilt based on their race, ethnic origin, or socioeconomic level. Prejudice is subtle and deeply ingrained in our sin nature. We must consciously work to expose it in our thinking and root it out of our lives.

> God in heaven, give us courts that work efficiently to protect the rights of the poor and powerless. At a deeper level, give us a legal system that overcomes the forces of greed and prejudice. Help me to confront the greed and prejudice in my life so that I may shine a light of truth and fairness in my world. Amen.

Look Ahead to Where Your Choices Are Leading

Proverbs urges us to consider the end result of a life of integrity and a life of dishonesty. As you make choices, look far ahead to where those choices will lead you.

> Whoever walks in integrity walks securely,
> but whoever takes crooked paths will be found out. (Proverbs 10:9)

Crooked paths will be discovered. Marilee Jones, dean of admissions at MIT, became well-known for her book on college admissions entitled *Less Stress, More Success*. It contained this advice: "Holding integrity is sometimes very hard to do because the temptation may be to cheat or cut corners. But just remember that 'what goes around comes around,' meaning that life has a funny way of giving back what you put out." This proved true in her life. Jones resigned her position after admitting she had lied on the resume she had submitted twenty-eight years earlier. She had claimed to have degrees from three New York colleges but had no degrees from anywhere.[11]

Deceit will eventually destroy you:

> The integrity of the upright guides them,
> but the unfaithful are destroyed by their duplicity. (Proverbs 11:3)

For years Bernie Madoff lived a life of luxury based on a Ponzi scheme. Eventually his deceit was discovered and he was sent to prison. Not every person who cheats or lies will be discovered in this life. Remember that the proverbs are wise sayings and are not absolute statements. Some liars and cheats get by with it in this life, but they will give an account on Judgment Day.

> Lord, help me see where my choices are leading me. If a pattern of
> deceit is forming in my life, give me the courage to admit it and
> turn from it now before it destroys me. Amen.

There is Power to Change

The New Testament continues the emphasis on the importance of honesty. When God was preparing the world for the coming of his Son, Jesus, he sent John the Baptist to call people to repentance. John's preaching contained a heavy emphasis on honesty:

> Even tax collectors came to be baptized. "Teacher," they asked, "what should we do?" "Don't collect any more than you are required to," he told them. Then some soldiers asked him, "And what should we do?" He replied, "Don't extort money and don't accuse people falsely—be content with your pay." (Luke 3:12–14)

The good news of Jesus offers not only the command to be honest but also the power to become an honest person. Even the worst thieves and swindlers can be forgiven and can find the power to change through Jesus Christ. When Jesus went to Jericho, he met a wealthy tax collector named Zacchaeus. This man had a reputation for being dishonest. Jesus showed kindness to Zacchaeus and became a guest in his home. Jesus's opponents criticized his association with this swindler. Zacchaeus was moved by Jesus's grace to him. He vowed to give half his possessions to the poor and promised to repay fourfold anyone he had cheated. Jesus responded, "Today salvation has come to this house, because this man, too, is a son of Abraham" (Luke 19:9).

> Jesus, thank you for loving me in spite of my lack of complete honesty. May your grace and goodness overwhelm me as it did Zacchaeus. I want salvation to come to my house. Transform me into a person of integrity by your indwelling Spirit. Amen.

Self-Control Is Like a Wall of Protection

Like a city whose walls are broken through
is a person who lacks self-control.
—Proverbs 25:28

Proverbs says there are two choices in life—righteousness or wickedness, the right way or the wrong way. We are looking at some of the individual choices within that theme. This week we consider the choice between self-control and drunkenness. Proverbs says self-control is like the wall that protects a city. When we are out of control, our defenses are down; enemies can invade our lives, and we can be destroyed.

The Bible says that we have a spiritual enemy, the devil. "Be alert and of sober mind. Your enemy the devil prowls around like a roaring lion looking for someone to devour" (1 Peter 5:8). The devil is looking for entry points into our lives. A sober mind alerts us to his attacks. When we lack self-control our guard is lowered, and he finds an opening.

What about your life? Are there areas where you are spiritually vulnerable because the walls are broken down? Is your thought life out of control? Is your spending out of control? Do you tend to lose control of your temper? The enemy will capitalize on these weak points in your spiritual defenses.

One bad choice that lowers our self-control is the excessive use of alcohol. This week we will study four passages in Proverbs that warn of the dangers of alcohol abuse.

> Dear God, often when our lives are out of control, we are the last people to realize it. Help me this week to examine my life honestly and to recognize areas where I am out of control. Thank you, Lord. Amen.

Alcohol Diminishes Your Self-Control

Wine is a mocker and beer a brawler;
whoever is led astray by them is not wise.
—Proverbs 20:1

Alcohol creates conflict in your life and causes you to make unwise choices. Distillation of hard liquor had not been invented in biblical times. Wine and beer are mentioned here. Even these fermented drinks with lower alcohol content are the object of warning. They are mockers and brawlers. This could mean they mock you and beat you up. More likely it means they turn you into a mocker (the worst kind of fool) and a brawler (a person who gets into fights and quarrels).

Alcohol is a mocker. Noah was a righteous man, blameless among the people of his time, and he walked faithfully with God (Genesis 6:9). Yet, when he drank too much wine and became drunk, he lay naked in his tent, and his sons had to cover him up (Genesis 9:21–23). Alcohol mocks even the righteous.

Alcohol is a brawler. Why do fights often break out in bars? Why is it you don't often hear of fights breaking out in libraries or movie theatres? Similar numbers of people gather at those places, but a difference is the absence of alcohol consumption.

Domestic violence is the leading cause of injury to women ages fifteen to forty-four. Drinking precedes 55 percent of domestic violence cases.[12] The theme of Proverbs is wisdom. Being led astray by alcohol is not wise. It clouds clear thinking and causes you to make choices that are not wise.

> Lord, has the use of alcohol become a problem in my life? Are any of the conflicts in my life fueled by my dependence on alcohol? If so, Lord, help me to see my problem clearly and to deal with this danger in my life. Thank you, Lord. Amen.

Alcohol Abuse Often Leads to Poverty

Listen, my son, and be wise,
and set your heart on the right path:
Do not join those who drink too much wine
or gorge themselves on meat,
for drunkards and gluttons become poor,
and drowsiness clothes them in rags.
—Proverbs 23:19–21

How do you keep your heart on the right path? Don't join with those who drink too much wine. Choose your friends and companions carefully. I urge college freshmen to consider carefully whether to pledge a fraternity. Binge drinking is a big problem on college campuses. Eighty-six percent of fraternity house residents binge drink, compared to 52 percent of those who live in a coed dorm, 40 percent of those who live off campus, and 38 percent who live in single-sex dorms.[13] Find other avenues to make friends that do not center on the consumption of alcohol.

This passage warns that drunkenness (and gluttony, another example of the lack of self-control) often leads to poverty. Just before I typed these words, I was on the phone calling halfway houses in our area. As I write this, a man in our church is getting out of jail, and he has nowhere to go. He has a continuing problem with alcohol abuse. Because of alcohol, he has lost a good job, a nice apartment, his relationship to his family, and the opportunity to drive. Now he has nothing, and he is trying to start over. Tragically, these verses in Proverbs chronicle his life.

> Lord, are there relationships in my life that are detrimental to my self-control and my pursuit of your plan for my life? Help me to be wise in my choice of friends and companions. Help me discern whether my choices in life have impacted my finances and caused me to be a poor steward of the opportunities and resources you have given me. Amen.

Alcohol Is Addictive and Self-Destructive

Who has woe? Who has sorrow?
Who has strife? Who has complaints?
Who has needless bruises? Who has bloodshot eyes?
Those who linger over wine,
who go to sample bowls of mixed wine.
Do not gaze at wine when it is red,
when it sparkles in the cup,
when it goes down smoothly!
In the end it bites like a snake
and poisons like a viper.
Your eyes will see strange sights,
and your mind will imagine confusing things.
You will be like one sleeping on the high seas,
lying on top of the rigging.
"They hit me," you will say, "but I'm not hurt!
They beat me up, but I don't feel it!
When will I wake up
so I can find another drink?"
—Proverbs 23:29–35

This passage is a graphic description of the physical and emotional toll of alcohol abuse. Alcohol causes sorrow, strife, and complaints. It leads to needless bruises (from fights? from running into things?) and bloodshot eyes. Alcohol is enticing and hypnotic, but in the end it is deadly. It causes delusions. It brings nausea akin to seasickness. It dulls the senses, and it leaves one wanting more.

The passage warns us not to linger over wine or to sample mixed wine. Mixed wine was wine mixed with spices, which was especially intoxicating. Wine mixed with myrrh was offered to Jesus on the cross, but he refused it, presumably in order to keep a clear head (Matthew 27:34).

> God in heaven, has my use of alcohol become destructive in my life? Am I addicted? Help me to be honest with myself and with you. Enable me to cut through my rationalizations and justifications. My life is laid bare before you. You see me as I really am. Thank you that you still love me. Lift me up out of the mess I have made. Thank you, Lord. Amen.

Leaders Are to Abstain from Alcohol

The sayings of King Lemuel—an inspired utterance his mother taught him.
Listen, my son! Listen, son of my womb!
Listen, my son, the answer to my prayers!
Do not spend your strength on women,
your vigor on those who ruin kings.
It is not for kings, Lemuel—
it is not for kings to drink wine,
not for rulers to crave beer,
lest they drink and forget what has been decreed,
and deprive all the oppressed of their rights.
Let beer be for those who are perishing,
wine for those who are in anguish!
Let them drink and forget their poverty
and remember their misery no more.
—Proverbs 31:1–7

This chapter was written by King Lemuel. It contains advice his mother gave him. She told her son that leaders should not drink alcohol. Leaders have great responsibility for those in their charge, and they need clear heads in order to govern or lead wisely. This passage says that beer and wine are intended as a painkiller or anesthetic for those who are perishing or in anguish.

If you are in a position of leadership, you should consider the advice of King Lemuel's mother. Some will consider this advice to be overly rigid or legalistic. Most commercial airlines have a rule that pilots are to abstain from the consumption of alcohol twelve to twenty-four hours before they pilot a flight. Most of us would not consider those rules as "overly rigid" or "legalistic." We are grateful for those policies, because we recognize that our lives may be at stake. Leadership carries with it great responsibility, including the responsibility to be clearheaded and in control.

Lord, help me to take seriously my role as a leader in my home,
my church, and my community. Forgive me if my example has led
anyone astray. Help me to keep a clear mind in all circumstances.
Give me the strength to be a wise, sober, consistent leader. Amen.

Jesus Offers a Fresh Start

Let us behave decently, as in the daytime, not in carousing and
drunkenness, not in sexual immorality and debauchery, not in dissension
and jealousy. Rather, clothe yourselves with the Lord Jesus Christ,
and do not think about how to gratify the desires of the flesh.
—Romans 13:13–14

The person you have been in the past does not have to be the person you will be in the future. The New Testament tells us that if you "put on" the Lord Jesus Christ, you can "put off" drunkenness and other enslaving sins.

Augustine was born in North Africa in AD 354. During his early years, he lived a life of immorality and excess rather than self-control. His mother, Monica, was a Christian, and she prayed for her son. Augustine was a brilliant man, and he viewed Christianity as a religion for the simple-minded. Augustine spent time in Milan, where he heard the preaching of Ambrose, the bishop of Milan. That preaching led Augustine to a new understanding of the Bible and Christianity. In the summer of AD 386, as Augustine sat in a garden, he heard a child's voice singing the words, "Pick it up and read it; pick it up and read it." He felt this might be God's way of speaking to him. He located a Bible and opened it. His eyes fell on Romans 13:13–14, the passage printed above. Augustine felt his heart flooded with light. He turned from his sin and was later baptized by Ambrose. Augustine went on to become one of the greatest church leaders in the history of Christianity. Jesus is able to produce a new beginning in your life.

Lord Jesus, I want to put off the sins of my life. I want to be
clothed in you. I want a fresh start in my life. Thank you, Jesus.
Amen.

The Holy Spirit Produces Self-Control

When you receive Jesus as your Savior, he sends his Holy Spirit to live inside your body. This is the presence of Christ within you to encourage you and to enable you to live a life that pleases God. So you are not alone in your battle to exercise self-control. As you keep in step with the Holy Spirit, he will produce the Christ-like life within you. Negatively, he will help you resist the temptation of alcohol: "Do not get drunk on wine, which leads to debauchery. Instead, be filled with the Spirit" (Ephesians 5:18). Positively, he will begin to produce his fruit within you, including the fruit of self-control:

> So I say, walk by the Spirit, and you will not gratify the desires of the flesh … The acts of the flesh are obvious: sexual immorality, impurity and debauchery; idolatry and witchcraft; hatred, discord, jealousy, fits of rage, selfish ambition, dissensions, factions and envy, drunkenness, orgies, and the like. I warn you, as I did before, that those who live like this will not inherit the kingdom of God. But the fruit of the Spirit is love, joy, peace, forbearance, kindness, goodness, faithfulness, gentleness, and self-control. Against such things there is no law. (Galatians 5:16, 19–23)

Developing self-control is like gardening. Suppose you want to grow watermelons. You plant a seed, and soon you have a vine with a tiny watermelon attached to the end of that vine. How do you encourage that watermelon to grow? You do not apply water and fertilizer to the little melon itself. You apply water and fertilizer to the root of the vine. When the root is nourished, it will send nutrients into that little melon, and it will grow. You do not build self-control by trying harder to be in control. You build self-control by nurturing your relationship with Christ, whose Spirit lives within you. Focus on the root to grow the fruit!

> Lord Jesus, I empty myself of any known sin. Fill me with your Holy Spirit. Holy Spirit, produce your fruit of self-control in my life. I pray in Jesus's name, Amen.

Patience and Anger

The wise fear the LORD and shun evil,
but a fool is hotheaded and yet feels secure.
—Proverbs 14:16

We are looking at some of the specific choices between righteousness and wickedness. We have examined the choice between honesty and dishonesty and the choice between self-control and drunkenness. Now we look at the choice between anger and patience. Do you ever get angry? I have had a problem with anger. I think the root of some of my anger is perfectionism. I tend to want everything to work perfectly. I want lawnmowers to crank, and computers to work, and cable TV to have a picture. I can identify with the man in Spring Hill, Tennessee, who shot his car. His 1988 Oldsmobile quit on the side of Saturn Parkway. He got out, took out his automatic rifle, and emptied three thirty-round clips into the side of his car![14]

Some of you have anger that comes from disappointment with your life or frustration with your job. Perhaps anger has become the normal way you interact with your spouse or your kids. You are always mad at the world and always yelling at someone.

Several years ago, I decided to do something about my anger. I looked up all the verses in Proverbs on anger, wrote them down in my prayer notebook, and memorized them. I believe there is therapeutic power in the Word of God. Maybe you need to learn what Proverbs says about anger.

Lord, this week I will try to absorb what your Word has to say about anger. Show me how my anger may be preventing me from enjoying the life you want me to have. Thank you, Lord. Amen.

Anger Makes You Act Foolishly

A quick-tempered person does foolish things,
and the one who devises evil schemes is hated.
—Proverbs 14:17

Whoever is patient has great understanding,
but one who is quick-tempered displays folly.
—Proverbs 14:29

Anger makes you do and say foolish things. The Hebrew word for anger in Proverbs is the word for *nose* or *nostril*. It conveys the idea of snorting in anger. The word *quick-tempered* is a compound of two words, literally *short-nosed*. The quick-tempered person is quick to snort. The word *patient* is literally *long-nosed*, or slow to snort. Are you a short-nosed or long-nosed person?

Not all anger is sinful. Some things should make us angry. Jesus got angry. But we should not be quick to be angry. Anger neutralizes our self-control and makes us act foolishly. A man in Homestead, Florida, went to the drive-through at his bank to make a withdrawal. He and the teller had a lengthy discussion about a check that had not cleared. As the discussion progressed, he became more and more irritated. The teller told him he would have to see the manager inside, but the inside was closed. At that point he pulled out of the drive-through and drove his truck through the glass doors at the front of the bank. He parked his truck and walked into the manager's office. When the police arrived, he was sitting at the manager's desk. He never got his money.[15] You have probably never done anything that drastic, but there may be times in your life when you acted foolishly because of your anger. It's embarrassing. It needs to change.

> Lord, I confess that I have sometimes acted foolishly because of
> my anger. I ask you to forgive my sin. I don't want to be like that
> anymore. I ask you to help me learn new ways of dealing with my
> anger. Amen.

Anger Leads to Other Sins

An angry person stirs up conflict,
and a hot-tempered person commits many sins.
—Proverbs 29:22

The one who has knowledge uses words with restraint,
and whoever has understanding is even-tempered.
—Proverbs 17:27

Here is another pair of Hebrew words in Proverbs for anger. The angry person is hot-tempered, or literally *hot-spirited*. The patient person is even-tempered, or literally *cool-spirited*. Are you a hot-spirited or cool-spirited person?

Anger is a trigger sin in your life. A hot spirit leads to problems in other areas of your life. Anger causes conflict in your relationships. Think about the relationship problems that you are having right now in your marriage, with your parents, or in your job. Do any of these conflicts have their roots in unresolved anger in your life? Is there resentment, frustration, or bitterness that is fueling your reactions and your moods? Perhaps you have been dealing with only the surface issues of these problems. Perhaps you need to look deeply in your life and ask, "What is the root of this frustration and resentment?" If you try to pull a dandelion out of your lawn, you will probably break off the tap root deep in the ground, and the plant may grow back. If you want to stop dandelions, you have to dig deeply and remove the root. If you want to get rid of the relational conflicts with which you struggle, you may need to dig deeply and address the anger in your life. A New Testament book of wisdom says: "Human anger does not produce the righteousness that God desires" (James 1:19).

> Dear God, I see now that my anger has led me into sin. I ask you to forgive me. I ask you to deal with the root causes of conflict and hatred in my life. Change my heart so that my attitude and words and actions may be transformed. Amen.

Overlook Small Offenses

A person's wisdom yields patience;
it is to one's glory to overlook an offense.
—Proverbs 19:11

What can you do to become patient (long-nosed) and even-tempered (cool-spirited)? Learn to overlook small offenses. Anger becomes a problem when we dwell on minor offenses and replay them in our minds. Don't be hypersensitive. Shrug off insults. Give grace. Years ago, I pastored a church in a rural community. There were two senior adult women in the church who were good friends. Then something happened, and it became obvious they were not as close anymore. I asked one of them about it. She told me that she had given her friend some cabbage from her garden. Her friend had said, "Thank you for the little cabbages." She was insulted that the woman had referred to her cabbages as "little." She took that as an insult. I was astounded. I tried to suggest that she might not have meant it that way. I suggested she focus on the words *thank you* rather than the word *little*. That disagreement seems silly, doesn't it? Yet, relationships are often broken by perceived insults that may have never been intended.

You do not need to talk to someone about every offense. If a relationship has already been damaged by anger, you will need to talk to that person and try to repair the relationship. But you do not have to tell a person every time you are hurt or angry or slighted. By the grace of God, let it go. It is to your glory to overlook an offense.

> Lord, help me to show the same grace to others that you have shown to me. Enable me to stop dwelling on small offenses, slights, and insults. Help me to put them out of my mind and let go of my anger. Thank you, Lord. Amen.

Anger Is Contagious

Do not make friends with a hot-tempered person,
do not associate with one easily angered,
or you may learn their ways
and get yourself ensnared.
—Proverbs 22:24–25

A second thing you can do to avoid a problem with anger is to carefully choose the people with whom you socialize. Anger is contagious. Some people have developed a pattern of responding to difficult situations with angry outbursts. These people are always in a rage about something. If you spend a lot of time in that kind of environment you may develop that same pattern of life. Studies have found that we often tend to unconsciously mimic the emotional expressions of others. Mimicry of a frown or a smile triggers reactions in our brains that cause us to interpret those expressions as our own feelings. "Simply put, as a species, we are innately vulnerable to 'catching' other people's emotions."[16]

While you cannot choose your family or your work associates, you can choose the friends who will influence you at a deep level. Be gracious and friendly to everyone, but do not form deep friendships with those whose basic approach to life is to be angry about everything. Instead train yourself to expect delays and irritations. Train yourself to look for humor, unexpected beauty, and instances of goodwill in the world around you. You can affect your circle of friends and create an environment that is positive, patient, and joyful.

> Lord, give me discernment in my choice of friends. Send me a friend who will support me in my desire to live life as you intended it. Forgive me if I have been a negative and hot-tempered influence in my circle of friends. Teach me your ways. Amen.

Learn to Restrain Your Anger

Fools give full vent to their rage,
but the wise bring calm in the end.
—Proverbs 29:11

Better a patient person than a warrior,
one with self-control than one who takes a city.
—Proverbs 16:32

The final strategy for overcoming an anger problem is to learn to exercise restraint. You can never avoid all situations that give rise to anger. You must develop some inner resources.

A literal translation of this verse might read, "The fool sends forth all his spirit, but the wise man holds back and quiets his spirit." Restrain your spirit. You do not have to say everything that comes into your mind. Words cause lasting damage. Married couples need to learn to discuss problems without verbal jabs and insults that cause lasting damage to the relationship.

Dwight D. Eisenhower had an explosive temper as a child. Once when his parents did not let him do what he wanted, he banged his fists into an apple tree until they bled. His father sent him to his room. His mother came and bandaged his hands. While she was applying the bandages, she quoted Proverbs 16:32 to him. He decided then that he would control his anger, and his anger would not control him. This lesson equipped him to maintain self-control as a general in World War II and as president of the United States. Many years later Eisenhower wrote, "I have always looked back on that conversation as one of the most valuable moments of my life."[17]

Lord, too often I have given full vent to my rage. I want to learn to be in control. Help me know how to quiet my spirit and restrain my anger. Amen.

The Holy Spirit Produces Patience

How do you learn to control your temper and develop patience? Even memorizing these proverbs is not enough. You need the Spirit of God. Once again, we need to consider the teaching in the New Testament book of Galatians. The acts of the sinful nature include fits of rage (Galatians 5:20), but the fruit of the Spirit include patience and self-control (Galatians 5:22–23).

Two things need to happen in your life for you to grow in patience and self-control. First, you die to the old nature. "Those who belong to Jesus have crucified the flesh with its passions and desires" (Galatians 5:24). This is a decisive action, making such a radical break with your past way of life that it is described as dying. You choose to join your life with Jesus, participating with him in the crucifixion of the flesh. This union is symbolized in baptism.

Second, you live by the Spirit, keeping in step with him. "Since we live by the Spirit, let us keep in step with the Spirit" (Galatians 5:25). This is a continuing action. When you are united with Jesus, his Spirit comes into your life to empower you. Then you must continually walk in the fellowship and power of the Spirit. That means an awareness of him and a daily dependence on his strength. Imagine learning to keep in step with a marching band or a military unit. At first it requires conscious effort to stay in step. Eventually, you develop a sense of rhythm, and the cadence becomes almost automatic. The same is true of keeping in step with the Spirit in your daily life.

> Dear Jesus, I have been joined with you by faith in your death and resurrection. I have died to my old way of life. I now treat my old desires as dead. Holy Spirit, I thank you that you are in my life. Help me to be aware of your presence and to walk in step with you today. Amen.

Peace and Quarreling in Your Home

Within the megatheme of righteousness and wickedness we have been looking at specific components of the right and wrong way to live. This week we will look at the choice between peace and quarreling.

> Better a dry crust with peace and quiet
> than a house full of feasting, with strife. (Proverbs 17:1)

The word "strife" in this verse represents a Hebrew word that is translated at least five different ways in Proverbs: "quarreling," "dissension," "disputes," "strife," and "conflict." This proverb is about conflicts in your house. Think about the level of conflict or peace in your home. Are you always fighting or arguing? One of the best gifts you can give your children is a stable home that is a place of security, refuge, and peace. You can choose the spiritual temperature in your home. Consciously work to set the thermostat toward calm and quiet rather than strife and quarreling.

This is one of several proverbs that begin with the word *better*. Life's choices involve tradeoffs. These type proverbs show the better choice. If you have to choose between either prosperity with strife or peace with poverty, it is better to trade prosperity for peace.

> Lord, I want my home to be a place of peace and quiet. I want to create an environment of harmony for my children. I want to give them a model of affirming relationships. I can't do that without your help. Calm my heart and enable me to be an advocate for peace in my home. Amen.

Is Your Marriage Characterized by Quarreling?

> Better to live on the corner of the roof
> than share a house with a quarrelsome wife.
> —Proverbs 21:9

Here is another of the "better" proverbs about peace in a home. The flat roof of an Israelite home was used as a patio. Better to move up there permanently than share space with a quarrelsome wife! Remember that these proverbs were written to young men preparing for life and marriage. Girls can change this to a quarrelsome husband. If that spouse is both quarrelsome and ill-tempered, the rooftop is not far enough away. Better to live in the desert:

> Better to live in a desert
> than with a quarrelsome and nagging wife. (Proverbs 21:19)

What is the conversation like between you and your spouse? Is it critical, competitive, and often negative? Does every discussion end in an argument? Consider this advice:

- Learn to listen without interrupting. Restate your spouse's point of view whether you agree with it or not. This will show you respect the person even if you disagree with the point of view.
- Choose carefully the words you speak to your spouse. Determine to say more positive things than negative things. Look for things you can affirm.
- Fight fair. Don't bring up past sins and arguments as additional ammunition. When you are so competitive that you try to win at all costs, you may win the argument but lose the relationship. Is winning worth the price?

Father in heaven, I ask for your help in my marriage. If I have been hard to live with, I ask your forgiveness. Enable me by your grace and power to become a different person and learn new ways to deal with conflict in my marriage. Amen.

Don't Be a Lover of Controversy

Whoever loves a quarrel loves sin;
whoever builds a high gate invites destruction.
—Proverbs 17:19

It is to one's honor to avoid strife,
but every fool is quick to quarrel.
—Proverbs 20:3

Everyone has conflict. Not all conflicts are your fault, and not all are sinful. Jesus was embroiled in conflict during his ministry. He was in conflict with the forces of evil. But much of our conflict is not like that of Christ. Much of our conflict is self-centered rather than kingdom-centered. If you are continually in quarrels and arguments at work, at home, and with friends, you may need to change some things in your life. What wisdom does Proverbs give us to minimize conflict and live at peace?

Proverbs warns us not to fall in love with drama and controversy. Some people love to stir things up. They love the attention that comes with conflict and drama. Proverbs says that to love a quarrel is to love sin. That is folly.

In the center of the Seal of the President of the United States is the image of an eagle. In its left claw the eagle clenches a bundle of arrows, a symbol of war. In its right claw the eagle holds an olive branch, a symbol of peace. Prior to the term of President Truman, the eagle's head was turned toward his left claw and the bundle of arrows. Truman wanted to emphasize peace. He had the seal modified so that the eagle's head is turned toward the olive branch in his right claw.[18] There will be both peace and conflict in our lives, but let us turn our heads toward peace.

Lord, am I quick to quarrel? Am I a lover of controversy? Help me to see myself as you see me. As far as it depends on me, I want to be a person of peace. Amen.

Don't Meddle in Other People's Quarrels

Like someone who grabs a stray dog by the ears
is someone who rushes into a quarrel not their own.
—Proverbs 26:17

Proverbs has some great word pictures. Imagine a large stray dog asleep in an alley. As you walk by on the sidewalk, would it be wise to go over and pull its ears? Probably not. It is just as foolish to meddle in a quarrel not your own. If you would choose a life of peace, avoid getting involved in controversies that do not concern you. This does mean Christians should avoid all controversies. You may be called to help a couple with their marriage problems even though that may become messy. Rather this means you exercise wisdom in choosing carefully those quarrels that require your involvement.

Once someone in the crowd said to Jesus, "Teacher, tell my brother to divide the inheritance with me." Jesus replied, "Man, who appointed me a judge or an arbiter between you?" Then he said to them, "Watch out! Be on you guard against all kinds of greed. Life does not consist in the abundance of possessions" (Luke 12:13–15). Jesus refused to get involved in this family dispute over an estate. He reserved his involvement for other "fights" to which God had called him. He would not be sidetracked from his primary mission.

Have you ever seen two boys wrestling and suddenly another child dives on the pile? He jumps into a fight that is not his own. Some Christians are like that. On social media, at church, or in our extended families, we jump into fights that are not our own. Wisdom produces discretion and restraint.

> Lord, forgive me if I have gotten sidetracked into minor squabbles
> that do not involve me and do not advance your kingdom work.
> Help me to be like Jesus and stay focused on the task to which
> you have called me. Amen.

What Are the Roots of Conflict in Your Life?

Another strategy for choosing peace over quarreling is to learn to discern the roots of conflict in your life. Why are you always quarreling with your parents or spouse? Why are you always in a conflict at work or school? We have already learned that Proverbs identifies anger as one root of conflict. Now we will identify four other potential roots of conflict in your life.

First, some conflict has its roots in hatred:

> Hatred stirs up conflict,
> but love covers over all wrongs. (Proverbs 10:12)

You may have been wronged by someone. Your desire is to get back at that person or to make him suffer. You want to hurt the one who has hurt you. Your hatred is hurting you more than him. You need to forgive. As hard as it is, you need to pray and ask God to help you love that person. Love covers offenses.

Second, some conflict has its roots in pride:

> Where there is strife, there is pride,
> but wisdom is found in those who take advice. (Proverbs 13:10)

We might also describe this as stubbornness. It is a refusal to take advice or to see any viewpoint but your own. Perhaps you have taken a strong issue on some position. There are some fair arguments for another viewpoint, but you have dug in your heels. To compromise or concede now would wound your pride. Your pride is causing conflicts in your life.

> Holy Spirit, shine your light deep within my heart and expose my
> hatred or pride. Change me in the very depths of my heart. Thank
> you, Lord. Amen.

What Are the Roots of Conflict in Your Life? (Part 2)

Today we continue to try to ferret out the roots of conflict in our lives. In addition to the root causes of hatred and pride, Proverbs identifies two others.

Third, some conflict is rooted in gossip:

> Without wood a fire goes out;
> without gossip a quarrel dies down. (Proverbs 26:20)

Gossip is repeating a rumor or private news (even if it's true). Gossip comes from a sense of insecurity. I know something you don't. If I share it, I will be the center of attention and will impress you. We sacrifice confidentiality to meet our emotional needs. Proverbs says many quarrels would die down if we would be quiet.

Fourth, some conflict is rooted in greed:

> The greedy stir up conflict,
> but those who trust in the Lord will prosper. (Proverbs 28:25)

Greed is the desire for more, no matter what we have. Give each of two kids a cookie, and one will complain, "His cookie is bigger than mine." The love of money is the root of all kinds of conflict. The other way to live is to trust God to prosper you.

What are the roots of conflict in your life? Will you ask God to help you be a person of peace?

> Lord God, I know that gossip and greed are easy to rationalize as
> concern and prudence. Cut through my rationalizations and show
> me my true motives and desires. Cleanse me, and then assure me
> of your love and forgiveness. Amen.

Peace with God Is Your Biggest Need

We need to go one step deeper to get to the real root of quarreling and strife in our lives. Ephesians 2 says the real source of human conflict is alienation from God. There is a conflict between us and God created by our rebellion against his authority. That conflict has spilled over into other relationships in our lives. God sent Jesus into the world to bridge the gap between us and God. His reconciling death on the cross also created the possibility for us to live at peace with one another:

> But now in Christ Jesus you who once were far away have been brought near by the blood of Christ. For he himself is our peace, who has made the two groups one and has destroyed the barrier, the dividing wall of hostility, by setting aside in his flesh the law with its commands and regulations. His purpose was to create in himself one new humanity out of the two, thus making peace, and in one body to reconcile both of them to God through the cross, by which he put to death their hostility. (Ephesians 2:13–16)

At the deepest level, you will not overcome the conflicts in your life until you deal with your alienation from God. Have you ever tried to paint over mildew? Paint covers it for a while, but then it reappears. You have to go deeper and deal with the problem at its source. When you are alienated from God, all your attempts to fix other relationships is like painting over the mildew. But when the center of your life is at peace, it creates the possibility for peace in all the other relationships in your life.

> Dear Jesus, thank you for putting to death my hostility to God through your death. Thank you for the sacrifice of your blood, which covers my sin and reconciles me to the Father. I rejoice that I am at peace with God! May the peace of God radiate through my life to all my relationships. Amen.

Megatheme 3: Relationships

The third megatheme in Proverbs is relationships. Proverbs gives practical wisdom for relating to God, your spouse, your children, your friends, and your neighbors. Two of these categories do not apply to everyone who reads this book: you may not be married, or you may not have children. You may choose to skip the section that does not apply to you. Or you may want to study that section if you anticipate either of those roles in your future or to help you understand others in your family or your church family. We will spend the next five weeks learning how to have a better life through better relationships.

You Can Have a Real Relationship with God

We begin our study of relationships with the most important relationship of all. You were made for a relationship with God. If you work on all your other relationships and ignore your relationship to God, you are like a doughnut—sweet on the perimeter but empty in the middle. You don't want to be a doughnut. You will never be whole until you come into a relationship with God.

For some people that phrase "relationship with God" sounds strange. God seems distant and unfathomable. The sayings of Agur are recorded in Proverbs 30, and he expressed some of this feeling:

> I have not learned wisdom,
> nor have I knowledge of the Holy One.
> Who has gone up to heaven and come down?
> Who has gathered up the wind? (Proverbs 30:3–4)

Sometimes a relationship with God seems as elusive as gathering up the wind. Yet, Proverbs talks about the possibility of a genuine connection with him:

> Have no fear of sudden disaster
> or of the ruin that overtakes the wicked,
> for the LORD will be at your side
> and will keep your foot from being snared. (Proverbs 3:25–26)

You can have a real a relationship with God, a daily relationship that involves communication, love, and sharing. The tough thing about a relationship with God is that you cannot see him or even directly hear him. It is a faith relationship. That lack of sight and sound does not preclude a relationship. I read of two women who were pen pals for fifty years. One lived in California and one in Maine. They started writing as eleven-year-olds in a school assignment. They met at age sixty-one. They had never seen each other, but they had a relationship for fifty years. God has written you a letter called the Bible. In it he invites you into a relationship with him.

> O God, I want a real relationship with you. I want to know you.
> I want a friendship with you. Teach me this week how to know
> you in a deeper way. Amen.

God Knows Everything about You

For your ways are in full view of the LORD,
and he examines all your paths.
—Proverbs 5:21

Proverbs says the basis for a relationship with God is that he already knows you. Some of you would like to get to know a famous actor or athlete or musician. The problem is that you know the celebrity, but he or she does not know you. You may be a fan, but you don't have a relationship because that person does not know you. However, the God who created the universe knows your name!

Proverbs says God knows all about you. Your ways are in full view of the Lord. We often think of God's omniscience in a negative way: he knows the bad things we are doing. Certainly, that should be a deterrent to evil in our lives. But God's omniscience is also a positive thing. It is the foundation for a real relationship. You can talk to God about anything in your life, because he is already familiar with your circumstances. He knows the complicated history of your relationships. He knows how you are feeling right now. Have you ever tried to talk to someone about a problem, but you soon got the feeling that person did not really understand the background of the problem or how you felt about it? God completely understands! There is no gap in his knowledge or understanding. No nuance escapes him. You never have to say to God, "It's complicated. You wouldn't understand."

Father, you know what is going on in my life right now. You know how I feel. Thank you for understanding me. It helps me to know that you are there, you are listening, and you care. Amen.

Learn What God Likes and Dislikes

To cultivate a relationship with God, learn what he likes and what he dislikes. That understanding is important to a relationship. My wife detests two things: coconut and glitter. If you deliberately serve her something with coconut in it without telling her, you will not develop a strong relationship with her. If you intentionally give her something covered in glitter, you will not endear yourself to her. I have a friend who dislikes heights. If you playfully nudge him when he is standing at an overlook, you will not develop a strong relationship with him. I like Mexican food. If you want to develop a relationship with me, suggest we go get some tacos.

What does God like and dislike? The book of Proverbs reveals what God likes and dislikes so that we can cultivate a relationship with him:

> The LORD detests dishonest scales,
> but accurate weights find favor with him. (Proverbs 11:1)

> The LORD detests lying lips,
> but he delights in people who are trustworthy. (Proverbs 12:22)

God abhors dishonesty, but he delights in integrity. Dishonesty will cause tension in your relationship with God because he abhors it. If you value a relationship with God, become a person of truthfulness. Honesty finds favor with God.

> Lord God, I recognize that my lack of honesty is offensive to you. Forgive me. I value my relationship with you more than any perceived benefits to my lying or deception. I want to become a person who can share a close relationship with you. Amen.

Learn That God Loves Authenticity

To cultivate a relationship with God, we need to learn what God likes and dislikes. Yesterday we learned that God dislikes dishonesty and lying, but he delights in integrity and truth. Today we continue to explore the preferences of God. The Lord detests insincere worship, but he delights in worship that is genuine:

> The LORD detests the sacrifice of the wicked,
> but the prayer of the upright pleases him. (Proverbs 15:8)

God cannot tolerate wickedness. His heart is drawn to righteousness:

> The LORD detests the way of the wicked,
> but he loves those who pursue righteousness. (Proverbs 15:9)

God is opposed to those who are arrogant and exalt themselves:

> The LORD detests all the proud of heart.
> Be sure of this: They will not go unpunished. (Proverbs 16:5)

God wants us to be real with him. He values transparency and humility. He detests hypocrisy and phoniness. These things are like fingernails on a chalkboard to God. Perhaps you don't feel close to God because you are doing things he detests and not doing things he likes.

> O Lord, how foolish of me to put up a front with you! You see through me. You know my thoughts and motives. Forgive me if I have been playing games with you. I want to come clean. I want to be real and honest with you. Thank you that you still love the real me. Amen.

Learn to Fear God

Indeed, if you call out for insight
and cry aloud for understanding,
and if you look for it as for silver
and search for it as for a hidden treasure,
then you will understand the fear of the LORD
and find the knowledge of God.
—Proverbs 2:3–5

If you want to know God, you must learn to fear him. We have already learned that the fear of the Lord is foundational to wisdom. Now we learn that the fear of the Lord is the key to knowing him. You may be thinking, *Fear does not sound like the basis of a healthy relationship.* It is when you are trying to get to know the one true holy God who breathed the stars into existence! You will not know him until you begin to understand his awesome holiness.

Timothy Treadwell wanted to get to know grizzly bears. So he camped among them in Alaska's Katmai National Park for thirteen summers. Treadwell tried to get close to the bears, even touching them and playing with bear cubs. Critics maintain that Treadwell lacked a healthy fear of the bears. He refused to carry bear spray. He clashed with the National Park Service because he refused to put an electric fence around his camp. The Park Service imposed a new rule, called the "Treadwell Rule," requiring campers to move their camps one mile every seven days. Treadwell initially complied but then hid his camp in heavy brush. In the fall of 2003, Treadwell extended his stay a week beyond his normal departure time, a time when limited food caused the bears to be more aggressive. He camped near a salmon stream in the midst of runways used by the bears. He was killed by a bear and eaten.[19] He could not continue the relationship he desired with the bears because he did not have a proper fear of them.

Do you fear the Lord? You will not know him until you are gripped by an awareness of his awesome holiness, righteousness, and power.

> O Lord Almighty, forgive me if I have treated you with the contempt that comes from familiarity. Forgive me if I have domesticated you and treated you as a pet whose role it is to please me and be my companion. I acknowledge that you are the One True Holy God. There is no one like you. You spoke the universe into existence. I bow in your presence. Amen.

Learn to Trust God

Whoever gives heed to instruction prospers,
and blessed is the one who trusts in the LORD.
—Proverbs 16:20

Fear of man will prove to be a snare,
but whoever trusts in the LORD is kept safe.
—Proverbs 29:25

If you want to know God, you must learn to trust him. Can you fear and trust someone at the same time? Yes, you can. Job did. Job experienced devastating loss in his life. He lost his family, his wealth, and his health. Job did not understand what God was doing in his life. God's ways seemed beyond understanding to him. Job questioned God. Yet, Job resolved, "Though He slay me, yet will I trust Him" (Job 13:15 NKJV). God will seem wild and mysterious at times. His ways will not always seem logical to your mind. You must decide if you can trust him even when you do not understand him. Have you seen enough of his character—his goodness and faithfulness—that you can trust him even when you do not understand him?

You will grow in knowledge of God as you learn to trust him more. Your trust will grow as you exercise little steps of faith. As you see God answer prayer and faithfully provide for your needs, you will learn that he is trustworthy. You will increasingly lean on his Word rather than on your own understanding. Proverbs says that trust in him will put you in a position where he can keep you safe.

Lord, I want to learn to trust you. My steps of faith may be
tentative and halting at first. Be patient with me. I want to learn
to trust you with all my heart. Amen.

You Can Know God through Jesus

Jesus has a unique relationship with God. He has known the Father for all eternity. John wrote of Jesus: "In the beginning was the Word, and the Word was with God, and the Word was God" (John 1:1). Jesus himself said, "I and the Father are one" (John 10:30). Jesus came to earth and became a human being to enable us to fully know God. He made the invisible God accessible to us. We know God by believing in Jesus:

> Jesus answered, "I am the way and the truth and the life. No one comes to the Father except through me. If you really know me, you will know my Father as well. From now on, you do know him and have seen him." Philip said, "Lord, show us the Father and that will be enough for us." Jesus answered: "Don't you know me, Philip, even after I have been among you such a long time? Anyone who has seen me has seen the Father. How can you say, 'Show us the Father?'" (John 14:6–10)

Placing your faith in Jesus brings knowledge of God, but that is only the beginning of a relationship with him. Some people think an initial conversion experience is all there is to knowing God. Instead, being born again is only the first chapter in a life of experiencing God. The apostle Paul became a follower of Jesus when he was a young adult. About thirty years later, when he was in his sixties, he wrote, "I want to know Christ—yes, to know the power of his resurrection and participation in his sufferings" (Philippians 3:10). Paul had a hunger to know God more and more. Do you have a hunger for a deeper relationship with God?

> Father, today I want to pray the prayer Paul taught us to pray in Ephesians 1:17: "I keep asking that the God of our Lord Jesus Christ, the glorious Father, may give you the Spirit of wisdom and revelation, so that you may know him better." Amen.

Choose a Person of Character for Your Spouse

Next to one's relationship to God, the marriage relationship is the most important in life. This week we will learn seven simple but extremely important marriage principles from Proverbs. First, Proverbs says to choose a person of character for your spouse:

> A wife of noble character is her husband's crown,
> but a disgraceful wife is like decay in his bones. (Proverbs 12:4)

Proverbs is written to young men who are not yet married. The first thing that will determine your happiness in marriage is the type person you select for a marriage partner. A spouse of noble character will crown your life, but a person without character can be like a cancer. So, determine that you will marry a person of character—a person of integrity, purity, trustworthiness, and wisdom. That means you will not choose a spouse based solely on physical appearance or attraction. God put that attraction in us, and it is good, but it is not to be the sole basis of selecting a marriage partner:

> Like a gold ring in a pig's snout
> is a beautiful woman who shows no discretion. (Proverbs 11:22)

You don't want to wake up every morning to a pig with a gold ring in its nose, do you?

How do you find a spouse of noble character? First, ask God to bring a godly person into your life. Have faith God will do it, and do not settle for less. Second, put yourself in situations to meet that kind of person. You aren't likely to find a steak dinner in a dumpster behind MacDonald's. You aren't likely to find a person of character in the bar scene. Third, be a person of noble character if you want to attract a person of noble character. A person of noble character is looking for someone with that same orientation in life.

> Dear God, send a person of noble character into my life. I will trust your timing in my life. I will not compromise my principles. Help me to be a person of noble character that such a person would want to marry. Amen.

View Your Marriage as a Covenant

Who has left the partner of her youth
and ignored the covenant she made before God.
—Proverbs 2:17

The context of this verse concerns a woman who commits adultery. I have already dealt at length with the subject of adultery, the greatest destroyer of marriage. I focus here on the view of marriage reflected in this verse. Here, marriage is described as a partnership and as a covenant relationship formed in the presence of God. Your attitude toward marriage has a great deal to do with whether it succeeds. Our culture has come to view marriage as only a legal contract that can be broken when it becomes unfulfilling. The biblical view is that marriage is a covenant made in the presence of God. It is a covenant like that which God makes with us—based on unconditional love and characterized by unbreakable loyalty. God says to those who come into a covenant relationship with him, "I will never leave you or forsake you" (Deuteronomy 31:6; quoted in Hebrews 13:5). In your marriage vows, you have made that same kind of covenant declaration to your spouse. View your marriage that way, and it will change your actions in your marriage.

Christopher Reeve, the actor who played Superman, fell from a horse and suffered a spinal injury that left him paralyzed from the shoulders down. In the days that followed, he considered pulling the plug on his life support. He told his wife, Dana, "Maybe we should let me go." His wife responded, "I want you to know that I will be with you for the long haul, no matter what. You are still you, and I love you."[20]

> Lord, help me view marriage as you view marriage. Help me to see
> it as a covenant relationship like the relationship I have with you.
> If I have been influenced by the world's perspective on marriage,
> forgive me, clarify my thinking, and give me a biblical outlook on
> marriage. Thank you, Lord. Amen.

Be Present in Your Home

Like a bird that flees its nest
is anyone who flees from home.
—Proverbs 27:8

Proverbs compares a man who strays from home to a bird that leaves its nest, abandoning the incubating eggs or baby birds. This proverb calls us to be physically and emotionally present in our homes. Invest your best in your home, and do not neglect your marriage.

Urban Meyer was the head football coach at the University of Florida. His job consumed him, and he neglected his family. When his daughter Gigi accepted a scholarship to play volleyball in college, she scheduled her signing ceremony around her father's schedule, consulting his calendar. Still, she didn't expect him to show up. When the day came, Meyer told his secretary he didn't have time to go. She insisted, "You're going." He finally joined his wife and daughter at a table in the school cafeteria. Gigi thanked her mother for being there season after season. Then she turned to her father. "You weren't there," she said. Her mom winced. Meyer went to his car and returned to work. Meyer's health began to suffer from his schedule. He had repeated chest pains, and he thought he was having a heart attack. He finally resigned as head coach at Florida. He began a season of soul-searching. A few years later he asked for his family's blessing to reenter coaching at Ohio State. They made him sign a contract before they would give their blessing. At his opening press conference, he read from the contract, written by one of his kids on pink notebook paper:

- My family will always come first.
- I will take care of myself and maintain good health.
- I will not go more than nine hours a day at the office.
- I will sleep with my cell phone on silent.
- I will continue to communicate daily with my kids.
- I will trust God's plan and not be overanxious.[21]

Lord, forgive me when I have been physically or emotionally absent from my home. Help me make the changes necessary in my schedule or my thoughts to be fully present in my home. Amen.

Choose Carefully How You Talk to Your Spouse

A quarrelsome wife is like the dripping
of a leaky roof in a rainstorm.
—Proverbs 27:15

The way you and your spouse talk to each other is a key factor in the strength of your marriage. Continuous quarreling is irritating, like the ceaseless dripping of a leaky roof. The issue is not so much whether you argue but how you argue. In his book *Blink,* Malcolm Glidewell describes the work of psychologist John Gottman. In his work with married couples, Gottman became adept at predicting which couples would divorce. He found that the key indicator was expressions of contempt. In his lab, spouses were connected with sensors that recorded physiological responses. Then they were asked to discuss some mildly contentious subject. The couples who got into arguments were not the ones most at risk. It was couples who put one another down or rolled their eyes at one another. Gottman found that chronic contempt suppressed the immune system. Spouses who live with chronic contempt tend to get more colds than those whose arguments do not involve contempt.[22] When marriage becomes a competition, contempt and put-downs become weapons for gaining an advantage. When we humble ourselves, we no longer need to express a position of superiority.

Is the way you talk to your spouse undermining the strength of your marriage? You can break your pattern of contempt and learn new ways of speaking to your spouse. Make a conscious effort to say something positive and affirming to your spouse each day. Look for opportunities to express appreciation to your spouse rather than focusing solely on flaws and deficiencies.

> Lord, I don't want to be like the dripping of a leaky roof in a
> rainstorm. Forgive me for needless quarreling. Make me aware of
> any expressions of contempt in my conversations with my spouse.
> Change us by your power, I pray. Amen.

Don't Let the Pursuit of Money Destroy Your Marriage

The greedy bring ruin to their households,
but the one who hates bribes will live.
—Proverbs 15:27

Money is one of the greatest stress points in marriage. Greed is a monster that can consume your marriage. Here are seven things you can do to tame the greed monster in your home:

- Pool your finances and your debt. When you get married, it is no longer "my checking account" and "your debt." It is "our assets" and "our liabilities." Be a team.
- Simplify your lifestyle. Don't take on such a high mortgage or car payment that you will continually be stressed to meet your obligations. Learn to be happy with less.
- Monitor your balance between work and family. Ask your spouse if he or she thinks you are striking a good balance.
- Set some financial goals together. What are your dreams? Where do you want to be in five years? Money can be a unifying factor in your marriage when you work together for a common goal.
- Affirm the contributions of both spouses to your financial goals. Value the contribution of the stay-at-home mother or the spouse who earns less income.
- Commit yourself to financial integrity. Greed will tempt you to compromise your honesty in financial matters. Our proverb says, "The one who hates bribes will live."
- Put God first. Jesus said you can't serve both God and money. You will love one and hate the other. Give a tithe of your income to your church. That is the biggest blow you can strike against the greed monster in your marriage.

Dear God, has money or career become an idol in my life that is threatening the health of my marriage? I don't want to bring ruin to my household by my greed. I want to seek you first. I want money to be my servant and not my master. Amen.

Live So That God Can Bless Your Marriage

The LORD'S curse is on the house of the wicked,
but he blesses the home of the righteous.
—Proverbs 3:33

God wants to bless your marriage, but God will not bless wickedness. In order to receive God's blessing on your family, become a person God can bless. If you are having trouble in your marriage you may be asking the question, "What's wrong with me and my spouse?" when the question you should be asking is, "What's wrong with me and God?" The root of your marital conflict may be that you are not following God's commandments in your life. Your house is under the Lord's curse. Confess your sin and turn from any duplicity or wrongdoing in your life. Sin brings turmoil to a home, but righteousness brings stability.

The wicked are overthrown and are no more,
but the house of the righteous stands firm. (Proverbs 12:7)

The most important factor in your marriage is your spiritual life. What you may need most in your marriage is spiritual renewal. You need God in your marriage. Chip and Joanna Gaines, stars of the popular home improvement show *Fixer Upper*, seek to put Christ first in their family and in their business. Chip says his faith journey can be traced back to a decision his mother, Gayle, made in 1975. She attended a Billy Graham Crusade in Albuquerque and responded to the invitation to follow Christ. Her family life changed as a result. She and her husband made church attendance a priority. They got involved in a young couples' Sunday school class. This young woman's commitment changed the course of her family and laid a spiritual foundation for her son. Now Chip's family is experiencing the blessing of her commitment and continuing that legacy.[23]

Lord, help me see the root causes of the problems in my marriage.
Is there any wickedness in my life? I want to turn from my sin. I
want to be right with you so that I can be right with my spouse and
experience your blessing on our home. Thank you, Lord. Amen.

Build Your Marriage Up Rather than Tear It Down

The wise woman builds her house,
but with her own hands the foolish one tears hers down.
—Proverbs 14:1

Take an honest look at your marriage. What direction would you say your marriage is heading? Is it trending upward or downward? How are you contributing to or correcting that trend? Are your words and actions building your house or tearing it down?

If your marriage is trending downward, it is important that you recognize that trend early on while there is still time to turn things around. Many couples do not wake up and take action until their marriage has deteriorated, and they have drifted far apart. As a pastor I often have couples come to me for counsel when things have gotten really bad. I try to help, but often I think to myself, *Why did you wait so long to get help? Why didn't you take action before you both became so distant, embittered, and entrenched?* Be proactive in recognizing the direction of your marriage, and be proactive in building it up.

The New Testament says that Jesus gives us the pattern and the power to build up our marriages: "Wives, submit to your own husbands as you do to the Lord. For the husband is head of the wife as Christ is head of the church, his body, of which he is the Savior … Husbands, love your wives, just as Christ loved the church and gave himself up for her" (Ephesians 5:22–23, 25). Jesus's example of sacrificial love is our model for the marriage relationship. Wives are to submit to their husbands. That means to get on the same team as your husband. Don't work against him; work with him. Husbands are to love their wives with the kind of love Jesus demonstrated on the cross—active, self-giving, extravagant love.

> Father, help me to discern the direction of my marriage. Am I doing or saying anything that is tearing it down? I want to wisely build up my home. I need your help, Jesus, to act with humble, sacrificial love. Amen.

Teach Your Children How to Live

The next relationship we will consider is that of parents and children. The advice of Proverbs to parents and children can be gathered into three big themes. The first theme is teaching and listening. Parents are to teach their children, and children are to listen to their parents' teaching:

> Listen, my sons, to a father's instruction;
> pay attention and gain understanding.
> I give you sound learning,
> so do not forsake my teaching.
> For I too was a son to my father,
> still tender, and cherished by my mother.
> Then he taught me, and he said to me,
> "Take hold of my words with all your heart;
> keep my commands, and you will live. (Proverbs 4:1–4)

Parents are to pass on to the next generation what they have learned from their parents. What if you did not have wise, godly parents? Your job is a little tougher if you did not have that pattern to follow. However, you have the opportunity to start a new legacy and to change your family tree.

What are you supposed to teach your kids? The whole book of Proverbs is the instruction of fathers to their sons. So teach the main themes of Proverbs. The main theme is wisdom. Teach them to be wise by teaching them to fear the Lord. Teach your kids to respect and honor God. The second theme is righteousness. Teach your kids what is right and what is wrong. Two other themes we will survey later in this book are how to manage money and how to speak correctly. These are four key themes to teach your kids.

> Father, thank you for giving me my children. Help me to fulfill my responsibility to teach my children about you. Help me to be intentional and focused in this awesome opportunity. Amen.

Teach Your Children by Example

You teach by example as well as by words. The way to teach your children to fear the Lord is for you to fear the Lord:

> Whoever fears the LORD has a secure fortress,
> and for their children it will be a refuge. (Proverbs 14:26)

Children learn what to fear from their parents. They will pick up your fears. If you have an unhealthy fear of storms, it is likely they will be unduly frightened by storms. If you have a healthy fear of God, it is likely they will have a healthy respect for God.

The way you teach your children righteousness is for you to do right:

> The righteous lead blameless lives;
> blessed are their children after them. (Proverbs 20:7)

Your actions will carry even more weight than your words. If you tell your kids to be honest, but they hear you lie to your boss on the phone, they will hear your actions louder than your words. On the other hand, your actions can reinforce your words. If your children see you take a financial loss rather than compromise your integrity to make a profit, it will speak volumes to them.

The word *blameless* in Proverbs 20:7 does not mean perfection. Noah is described as being blameless, but the Bible makes clear that he was not the perfect parent. To be blameless means to be whole, sound, and upright. It means that no substantial charge can be leveled against one's character. You will not be perfect, but you can be blameless before your children. That is the way to bless them.

> Father, I want to live in such a way that I will be happy if my children become exactly like me. Teach me to fear you so that they will fear you. Help me lead a blameless life before them. Amen.

Aim Your Children in the Right Direction

Start children off on the way they should go,
and even when they are old they will not turn from it.
—Proverbs 22:6

Children are like arrows. You cannot control the flight of an arrow after it leaves your bow, but you can aim it in the direction you want it to go. Other factors may affect the course of the arrow in its flight (wind, obstacles in its path), but the aim is the single greatest factor in the trajectory of an arrow. This proverb says the single greatest factor in the outcome of your kids is the direction you point them.

This proverb can be misunderstood. It is not a guarantee. Parents of wayward kids want to claim it as a promise that their children will always come back, but that is not its intent. I have shared that the Proverbs are general statements of truth, not iron-clad promises. For example, we have already learned that Proverbs says wisdom brings long life and riches. That means wisdom gives the best chance of long life, but it is not an unconditional guarantee that you will live a long life. The same is true here. If this verse is a guarantee, then if your child turns from the right way when he is old, the only conclusion is that you did not train him correctly when he was young. That brings needless guilt to parents. The variable is your child's will. But the best chance for him to go the right way is for you to aim him in the right way. Children and arrows usually (but not always) go where they are aimed. Aim your children well. Do not place on yourself responsibility for their trajectory after they leave your bow.

Father, I want to give my children the best opportunity for a good and godly life. Help me to point them in the right direction while they are under my control. Thank you. Amen.

Children, Listen to Your Parents

If the first responsibility of parents is to teach their children, the first responsibility of children is to listen to their parents' teaching. Proverbs says this at least fifteen times. Let me share two examples:

> Listen, my son, accept what I say,
> and the years of your life will be many. (Proverbs 4:10)

> Listen to your father, who gave you life,
> and do not despise your mother when she is old. (Proverbs 23:22)

Accepting your parents' teaching gives you the best chance at a long life. Your pride will cause you to think that you are very different from your parents and that your problems and situations are different from theirs. However, humility and the Bible reveal that every generation experiences the same basic needs, dreams, and temptations. Because you are more knowledgeable about today's culture, your pride will cause you to think you are wiser than your parents. However, the Bible indicates that life lessons are distilled through time and experience. You will be blessed if you listen to your parents. Many young adults, intoxicated with their new-found independence, tend to spurn parental advice in their twenties, circle back to it in their thirties, speak fondly of it in their forties, and long for it in their fifties or sixties when it is no longer available.

> Father, help me to cherish the counsel of godly parents as one of
> your good gifts. Enable me to recognize my foolish pride and lay
> it aside so that I may really listen to them and to you. Amen.

Discipline Your Children

The second major theme in Proverbs about parents and children is discipline. Parents, discipline your children. Children, accept your parents' discipline:

> Discipline your children, and they will give you peace;
> they will bring you the delights you desire. (Proverb 29:17)

Proverbs advocates spanking as a method of discipline:

> Whoever spares the rod hates their children, but the one who
> loves their children is careful to discipline them. (Proverbs 13:24)

Some parents don't believe in spanking. Our culture is trying to link spanking to aggression in children and to child abuse. I was visiting Vanderbilt Children's Hospital. It was Child Abuse Prevention Month. In the food court there were promotional posters on each table that read: "Hitting or spanking never helps. It teaches children that hitting is OK." I challenge that assertion. We all hate child abuse and want to prevent it. If there was a direct correlation between spanking and child abuse, shouldn't the rate of child abuse be declining as fewer parents use spanking as a method of discipline? That is not the case. Our culture is losing the biblical balance between no discipline on one extreme and child abuse on the other. Proverbs links discipline to a love for children. We have abandoned spanking in part because we have abandoned the view of the sinful nature of human beings. Proverbs says folly is bound up in the human heart even in childhood:

> Folly is bound up in the heart of a child,
> but the rod of discipline will drive it far away. (Proverbs 22:15)

That viewpoint is not in vogue in our culture now. We must judge our opinions by the Word of God and not judge the Word of God by our opinions.

> Father, help me to love my children enough to discipline them.
> Give me wisdom concerning how to correct them. Help me be
> neither a permissive parent nor a harsh parent. Give me patience
> and persistence in dealing with a strong-willed child. May my
> children delight both me and you. Amen.

Children, Accept Your Parents' Discipline

If the duty of parents is to discipline their children, the duty of children is to accept their parents' discipline:

> A fool spurns a parent's discipline,
> but whoever heeds correction shows prudence. (Proverbs 15:5)

No one enjoys being corrected. When our behavior or attitude is challenged, our natural reaction is to become defensive. Our impulse is to justify our actions or attitudes. Our pride causes us to resist any correction. The humility that comes from wisdom will enable us to value our parents' discipline as evidence of their love for us. How we respond to the discipline of our parents prepares us to respond to the discipline of our heavenly Father. If we despise our parents' discipline, we will tend to resent the Lord's discipline in our lives. If we see our parents' discipline as evidence of their love, we will be able to appreciate our heavenly Father's correction in our lives:

> My son, do not despise the LORD'S discipline,
> and do not resent his rebuke,
> because the LORD disciplines those he loves,
> as a father the son he delights in. (Proverbs 3:11–12)

> Heavenly Father, forgive me when I have spurned my parents' discipline. Help me to overcome my pride and accept their correction as evidence of their love for me. Help me to realize that through them you are teaching me to submit to your discipline in my life. Amen.

Bring Joy to Your Parents by Your Life of Wisdom

The third theme of Proverbs concerning parents and children is that children bring joy to their parents by lives of wisdom:

> A wise son brings joy to his father,
> but a foolish son brings grief to his mother. (Proverbs 10:1)

> My son, if your heart is wise,
> then my heart will be glad indeed;
> my inmost being will rejoice
> when your lips speak what is right. (Proverbs 23:15–16)

> The father of a righteous child has great joy;
> a man who fathers a wise son rejoices in him.
> May your father and mother rejoice;
> may she who gave you birth be joyful! (Proverbs 23:24–25)

Parents, communicate to your children that their righteousness is your greatest joy and that their folly will be your greatest disappointment. Some parents communicate that achievement in sports or academics will be their greatest joy. They set expectations that children cannot meet. When I was in elementary school we received a letter grade for conduct as well as for academic subjects. (In my earliest grades, it was called "deportment," but that makes me sound really old.) I made good grades in the academic subjects, but on one report card I received a low grade in conduct. I can still remember my parents' negative reaction! I remember my dad saying something to this effect: "You may not always be able to achieve the best grades in academics, but you can control what you make in conduct." They were communicating to me that my righteousness was their greatest joy.

Are you bringing joy or grief to your parents by your character? Regardless of your "success" in life, godly parents will rejoice if your heart is wise and your lips speak what is right.

> Heavenly Father, I pray that I may live in such a way that those who gave me birth will rejoice in my character. Father, I want to value what you value. Help me to communicate to my family that their righteousness is my greatest joy. Thank you, Father. Amen.

Choose Your Friends Carefully

The righteous choose their friends carefully,
but the way of the wicked leads them astray.
—Proverbs 12:26

Among the most spiritually important relationships in your life are your relationships with your friends. Your friends will have a powerful influence on your thinking, your character, and your actions. Be selective in choosing the people who will exercise that influence upon you. For example, Proverbs warns not to become close friends with those who are easily angered (Proverbs 22:24–25) or those who tend to get drunk (Proverbs 23:20). Such behavior is contagious. Is the group of friends you hang out with encouraging or hindering your walk with God?

What can you do to choose your friends wisely?

- Pray. Perhaps you are on a team, in a dorm, or in a workplace where you do not have many friends who share your faith or values. Ask God to bring into your life someone who can encourage you and whom you can befriend. Then watch to see what God does. Parents, pray for the friends of your children. When my sons were growing up, I wrote down the names of their best friends in my prayer notebook and prayed for them when I prayed for my sons. I knew their friends would have a huge impact on their lives.
- Be the kind of person you want to attract as a friend. Bees are attracted to nectar, and flies are attracted to—well, never mind what flies are attracted to.
- Go to church. People in church are not perfect. Church people are sinners. But the best place to meet people who like cars is a car show. The best place to meet a cowboy is a rodeo. The best place to meet people who want to follow Jesus is a church. Get involved in your church's ministry and a side benefit will be new friendships.

Dear God, I want to be the person described in Psalm 1 who does not walk in step with the wicked or stand in the way that sinners take or sit in the company of mockers. I want to sit and stand and walk with people who delight in you. Amen.

Develop an Inner Circle and an Outer Circle of Friends

Walk with the wise and become wise,
for a companion of fools suffers harm.
—Proverbs 13:20

Proverbs warns about making the circle of our friendships too large and being led astray by those of questionable character. There is another extreme that is equally wrong: making the circle of our friendships too small and snubbing some people who need a friend. How do we balance these two extremes? As always, Jesus is our guide. Jesus had a wide outer circle of friends. He was criticized by some of the religious people of his day for his friendships with questionable characters (Matthew 9:10–12; 11:19). But Jesus also carefully chose those who were his close friends (Mark 3:13–14). He carefully chose twelve friends with whom he would share his life. Within the circle of twelve disciples he had an inner circle of three that he allowed to get even closer to him (Mark 5:37; 9:2; 14:32–33). Jesus did not give all people equal access to his life. Jesus models the biblical view of friendships: a wide outer circle and smaller inner circles.

Is your outer circle of friendships too narrow? We must have a wide outer circle if we would be like Jesus. We must befriend people of other religions and no religion and those whose lifestyles are different from ours.

Is your inner circle of friendships too wide? Proverbs warns it is dangerous to allow people close to you who do not share your values or direction in life. Exercise equality in respect but not equality in access. It is especially important to choose friends carefully when you enter a new phase of your life—when you begin college or move to a new city or begin a new job. Initial friendships in these new settings will often be especially influential in your life, as you are eager for camaraderie and affirmation.

> Lord Jesus, help me to broaden my circle of friends to include people who are different from me. Forgive me if I have shunned someone created in your image. At the same time, forgive me if I have become a companion of fools. Help me to seek out wise people to be my friends. Thank you, Jesus. Amen.

Allow Godly Friends to Sharpen Your Life

Perfume and incense bring joy to the heart,
and the pleasantness of a friend
springs from their heartfelt advice.
—Proverbs 27:9

As iron sharpens iron,
so one person sharpens another.
—Proverbs 27:17

One of the great joys of friendship is the advice and encouragement friends can provide. Proverbs says friendship is like the fragrance of perfume or incense. It is one of the gifts of God. We can benefit greatly from the perspective of friends.

How does God work in our lives to transform us into his image? Christians would probably answer that God works through the Holy Spirit and the Bible to transform us. That is certainly true, but God usually works through incarnation. That is, God works through people. The Holy Spirit speaks through the voice of people. People embody biblical truth. God wants to shape your life through your friendships, as iron sharpens iron. If you want to grow as a Christian, one of the most practical things you can do is ask a more mature Christian in your church to meet with you once a month or once a week to talk. Most will not volunteer to do that, but many will if you ask.

God also wants to use you to sharpen others. Howard Hendricks has compared this relationship to the apostle Paul, his partner Barnabas, and his apprentice Timothy. "Every disciple needs three types of relationships in his life. He needs a 'Paul' who can mentor and challenge him. He needs a 'Barnabas' who can come alongside and encourage him. And he needs a 'Timothy,' someone that he can pour his life into."[24]

> Lord, thank you for the wonderful gift of friends. Thank you for the mentors in my life. Help me to imitate their lives. Show me a younger person in my church or neighborhood whom I can befriend and encourage. Amen.

Accept Correction from Godly Friends

Wounds from a friend can be trusted,
but an enemy multiplies kisses.
—Proverbs 27:6

Enemies "kiss up" to you. A good friend will tell you the truth in love. Will you allow someone who loves you to tell you the truth, even to wound you? The Bible indicates that many of us have a distorted picture of our character. While we can spot sawdust in the eyes of others we are often unable to spot a plank of lumber in our own eyes (Matthew 7:3). Most of the time when Christians are about to do something stupid, there is someone who is warning them of the consequence of their actions. Most Christian men who have had affairs have ignored the wise counsel of friends who cautioned them that they were wrecking their lives and families. It takes humility to accept correction from friends.

The Hebrew word for *friend* in this verse is different from the word in other verses we have studied so far. This is the Hebrew word *ahab*, which means "one who loves you." You have to earn the right to wound a friend. I do not want people who do not love me to wound me. The way to be receptive to the correction of friends is to form strong relationships of accountability in advance. This is the value of a small group that enters a covenant to hold each other accountable and gives trusted friends permission to speak the truth even when it hurts.

Lord, help me to form strong bonds of friendship in my life. Give me the humility to listen to godly friends even when they wound me. Amen.

Be Loyal to Your Friends

A friend loves at all times,
and a brother is born for a time of adversity.
—Proverbs 17:17

One who has unreliable friends soon comes to ruin,
but there is a friend who sticks closer than a brother.
—Proverbs 18:24

Do not abandon your friends when they fail or make mistakes. That is when they need you most. Loyalty does not mean you cover for your friends when they do wrong or you make excuses for their transgressions. Loyalty means you do not desert your friends when they have problems.

One of the greatest examples of loyalty in the Bible is the story of David and Jonathan. David was a soldier and servant of Jonathan's father, Saul. Saul knew that God had chosen David to succeed him as king, and he was jealous of David for his military success. David was convinced that Saul wanted to kill him, but Jonathan had a hard time believing this was true of his father. Jonathan and David made a covenant of friendship, pledging their love and support to one another. Jonathan asked for David's kindness when he became king. He promised to warn David if his father expressed ill intentions toward him. David proposed a test. He would be absent from the upcoming New Moon feast. Jonathan would explain that David had a family obligation, and he would judge his father's reaction. When Jonathan delivered the news, Saul flew into a rage, pledged to kill David, and even threw a spear at his son. Jonathan met David at the arranged location and delivered the news. The two embraced and wept. They knew their relationship would not be able to continue as it had. Jonathan said to David, "Go in peace, for we have sworn friendship with each other in the name of the Lord" (1 Samuel 20:42). Such friendships should be highly prized.

Lord, thank you for loyal friends in my life. Help me be a friend who loves at all times, a friend who sticks closer than a brother. Amen.

Forgive Your Friends

Whoever would foster love covers over an offense,
but whoever repeats the matter separates close friends.
—Proverbs 17:9

All friendships will have some rough spots. There will be perceived slights and insults. Small differences can balloon into big problems and separate even long-standing friendships if we let them. This proverb calls us to cover over the offenses of our friends. This phrase means to "overlook" (MSG) offensive words and actions. When there is a large offense that is known to both you and your friend and is obviously affecting the relationship, you may need to talk about it openly and resolve it. However, you do not need to talk about every hurt or slight. You can simply overlook small offenses and forget about them. My grandmother used to say, "Let it go like water off a duck's back." A duck has a gland near the base of its tail that secretes oil. As the duck preens himself, he spreads this oil over his feathers creating a water-repellent surface. Water simply rolls off. In the same way, let minor offenses roll off you. Do not dwell on them or give them any place in your mind.

Our enemy, the devil, is a destroyer. He wants to destroy the relationships in our lives, including our friendships. God has given us two strategies to combat the enemy's plot to destroy our friendships. These strategies are love and forgiveness. God has modeled the use of these strategies toward us. He has loved us in spite of our transgressions against him, and he has forgiven our offenses. He calls us to follow his example.

> Lord, as you have forgiven me, help me to forgive the offenses of my friends. If the offense has already divided our relationship, help me to talk to my friend about it. If the offense is small or unknown to him, help me to cover it with love and resume our friendship. Amen.

Jesus Wants to Be Your Friend

There may be times in your life when you do not have any close friends. Perhaps you have just moved to a new area. Perhaps you are working in a place where there do not seem to be other people who share your outlook on life. You can have a friendship with Jesus. He is a real person who desires a personal relationship with you. He will be loyal to you when other friends desert you. He will sharpen you as iron sharpens iron. You have no reason to expect such a friendship, but he offers it to you: "Here I am! I stand at the door and knock. If anyone hears my voice and opens the door, I will come in and eat with that person, and they with me" (Revelation 3:20). Understand this is not a friendship of equals. He is the master, and you are his servant. But if you keep his commands, he promises a relationship that is far closer then master and servant:

> Greater love has no one than this: to lay down one's life for one's friends. You are my friends if you do what I command. I no longer call you servants, because a servant does not know his master's business. Instead, I have called you friends, for everything that I learned from my Father I have made known to you. (John 15:13–15)

In 1855 a man named Joseph Scriven sought to comfort his mother during a time of sorrow. He wrote a poem for her, which later became a much-loved hymn:

> What a friend we have in Jesus, all our sins and griefs to bear!
> What a privilege to carry everything to God in prayer.
>
> Do thy friends despise, forsake thee? Take it to the Lord in prayer;
> In his arms He'll take and shield thee; thou wilt find a solace there. [25]

Jesus wants to share life with you in daily fellowship. I can honestly say that my best friend is Jesus. I encourage you to get to know him.

> Jesus, I open the door of my life to you. I want to get to know you. I ask you to fill the loneliness in my life with your presence. I will seek to follow you. Thank you for calling me friend. Amen.

Be Mindful of Your Neighbors

Do not plot harm against your neighbor,
who lives trustfully near you.
—Proverbs 3:29

Better a neighbor nearby than a relative far away.
—Proverbs 27:10

How do you relate to the people who live near you? Whether you live in a house, an apartment, or a dorm room, you have neighbors. The Hebrew word in Proverbs for *neighbor* is the same word as *friend*. It refers to a person with whom you associate. When it is association by choice, it is translated *friend*. When it is association by location, it is translated *neighbor*. Context determines the translation. Proverbs calls us to be mindful of those who live near us.

What kind of neighbor are you? When I moved to my town over twenty years ago, I did not know anyone. The first knock at our door was a couple from church carrying a cherry pie. They became great friends. The second knock at our door was from our next-door neighbors. I thought they had come to introduce themselves, so I invited them in. They stood at the threshold with somber looks. I soon learned they had come to ask me not to let my children run through their lawn anymore. I want to be like the first neighbor and not the second!

Many of us do not even know our neighbors. Our busy schedules cause us to drive by our neighbors with only a wave before we disappear into our homes. I encourage you to begin to do three things. First, meet your neighbors. Introduce yourself to the person who lives to the right and left of you. Second, pray for your neighbors by name. Third, watch for opportunities to be a good neighbor.

Lord, open my eyes to the people around me, the people across
the street, across the hall, or down the road. Help me to see them,
really see them, as you see them. Amen.

Be Considerate of Your Neighbors

If you find honey, eat just enough—
too much of it, and you will vomit.
Seldom set foot in your neighbor's house—
too much of you, and they will hate you.
—Proverbs 25:16–17

Like a maniac shooting
flaming arrows of death
is one who deceives their neighbor
and says, "I was only joking!"
—Proverbs 26:18–19

If anyone loudly blesses their neighbor early in the morning,
it will be taken as a curse.
—Proverbs 27:14

Each of these proverbs describes an action that is inconsiderate of neighbors. There is humor in this collection of proverbs. Showing up at your neighbor's house too often is compared to eating too much honey; both can be nauseating! Taking a joke too far is compared to shooting flaming arrows up into the air. Those arrows could fall on you! Making loud noise early in the morning is annoying, even if the noise is intended as a blessing.

Are you annoying your neighbors in any way? Do you let your pets run loose on their property? Do you play loud music at daybreak on Saturday morning? Do you get rid of your leaves by blowing them onto your neighbor's lawn? Sometimes we offend our neighbors without even thinking about it. These proverbs remind us that little things are important when you live in close proximity to someone. They call us to develop a sensitivity in our relationships with those around us.

Lord, help me to do nothing out of selfish ambition or vain conceit. Rather, in humility enable me to value others above myself. Help me to not look to my own interests but also to the interests of others. In my relationship with others, help me have the same mind-set as Christ Jesus, who humbled himself (Philippians 2:3–7). Amen.

Be Careful What You Say about Your Neighbors

Whoever derides their neighbor has no sense,
but the one who has understanding holds their tongue.
—Proverbs 11:12

Those who flatter their neighbors
are spreading nets for their feet.
—Proverbs 29:5

These two proverbs show the balance that characterizes godly wisdom. On the one hand, the wise are careful not to deride their neighbors. It makes no sense to insult or needlessly offend a person who is living by you every day. Several years ago an older lady moved into the house next door to us. A piece of furniture went missing during the move. She accused one of her neighbors of stealing the item during the transition. The police came to our door and questioned us about it. That's not the way to make a good first impression on your neighbors!

On the other hand, the wise do not engage in excessive flattery of their neighbors. The intent of flattery is to gain favor or advantage that can be exploited for gain at a later date. Proverbs says the flatterer is spreading a net that will later entrap his neighbor. Flattery is different from genuine appreciation and gratitude. The intent of flattery is to manipulate others for selfish reasons.

Lord, help me be wise in the way I speak to my neighbors. Help me not to speak in anger or impulsively and so damage our long-term relationships. Help me never to try to manipulate my neighbors but to treat them in the way I want to be treated. Amen.

Be Generous to Your Neighbors

The poor are shunned even by their neighbors,
but the rich have many friends.
It is a sin to despise one's neighbor,
but blessed is the one who is kind to the needy.
—Proverbs 14:20–21

Proverbs 14:20 is descriptive of how things are in our world: "The poor are shunned by their neighbors." Proverbs 14:21 is prescriptive of how God wants us to be: "Blessed is the one who is kind to the needy." Are you sensitive to the needs of those who live near you? Are there needs that God is calling you to meet in your neighborhood? If you are a follower of Christ, God has placed you where you live for a purpose. He has a purpose for you in your relationship with each of your neighbors. If he has placed wonderful Christian neighbors near you, it is to encourage and support you. If he has placed non-Christian neighbors near you, it is so that your life may reflect the love of Christ to them. If he has placed abrasive or inconsiderate neighbors near you, it is to help you grow and to teach you to love. If he has placed neighbors with financial difficulties near you, it is so that you can be a channel of blessing to help them.

The best kind of charity is local charity. National and international charity is needed, but it is more expensive, more difficult to monitor, and more easily abused. The best charity is when neighbors help neighbors.

Lord, forgive me if I have shunned or despised my neighbors because of their economic status. Guide me to know how I can use your resources to help my neighbors. Amen.

Set Appropriate Limits

One who has no sense shakes hands in pledge
and puts up security for a neighbor.
—Proverbs 17:18

The admonition to share with neighbors does not mean we are to do whatever they ask. Proverbs tells us to set appropriate limits on our relationships with our neighbors. Specifically, Proverbs says not to put up security for a neighbor. If your neighbor needs financial help, you may choose to give help. If you are unable or unwilling to give direct assistance, do not cosign a loan. This changes the relationship from that of neighbor to one of lender and borrower. If your neighbor is unable to pay, you will be responsible for the debt. If you have already become entangled financially with a neighbor, Proverbs says to extricate yourself immediately from the situation. The sense of urgency in this passage is clear:

> My son, if you have put up security for your neighbor,
> if you have shaken hands in pledge for a stranger,
> you have been trapped by what you said,
> ensnared by the words of your mouth.
> So do this, my son, to free yourself,
> since you have fallen into your neighbor's hands:
> Go—to the point of exhaustion—
> and give your neighbor no rest!
> Allow no sleep to your eyes,
> no slumber to your eyelids.
> Free yourself, like a gazelle from the hand of the hunter,
> like a bird from the snare of the fowler. (Proverbs 6:1–5)

Being generous to your neighbor does not mean that you enable bad behavior. With our children and with our neighbors, sometimes the best thing we can do for them is say no.

> Lord, help me to know when to say yes and when to say no to those around me. Help me not be gullible or manipulated by the plans of others. Give me wisdom and discernment to be prudent in my relationships. Amen.

Handle Conflict with Integrity

Do not testify against your neighbor without cause—
Would you use your lips to mislead?
Do not say, "I'll do to them as they have done to me;
I'll pay them back for what they did."
—Proverbs 24:28–29

Like a club or a sword or a sharp arrow
is one who gives false testimony against a neighbor.
—Proverbs 25:18

Whenever people live in close proximity to one another there will be misunderstandings and conflicts. Watch an afternoon of television court programming, and you will hear a variety of disputes about broken fences and leaking swimming pools and pet behavior. Christians are not exempt from conflict with neighbors. I know godly people who have found themselves the subject of lawsuits by their neighbors. Our challenge is to respond in a way that keeps us true to our faith and values. Conflict with neighbors can be a test that reveals the depth of our convictions. These proverbs warn us of two dangers in disputes with our neighbors. The first temptation is to seek revenge: "I'll pay them back for what they did." If a neighbor abuses my property, then I'll abuse theirs. If a neighbor makes noise late at night, I'll make even more early in the morning. The second temptation is to give false testimony, to exaggerate a neighbor's offense in court or in the court of neighborhood gossip. Let us view our small quarrels with neighbors as God's midterm exam. He uses these clashes to reveal our character flaws and to shape us into the image of Christ.

> Lord, help me to see your purposes even in the minor irritations in my life. Help me to handle conflict with integrity and Christ-likeness. Help me not to retaliate but to leave vengeance to you. Amen.

Love Your Neighbor as Yourself

What does the New Testament say about how to relate to our neighbors? Jesus said all the commandments can be summed up in two: love God with all your heart, and love your neighbor as yourself (Matthew 22:36–40). All of the commands in the Proverbs about neighbors can be summed up in the admonition to love our neighbors as ourselves.

Once a man asked Jesus, "Who is my neighbor?" This man wanted to define the circle of those he must love. He wanted to limit his "neighborhood" so that he could feel justified in not loving some people. Jesus would not allow him to narrow his definition of neighbor. Jesus told a story we call the Parable of the Good Samaritan. It is about three people who encountered a man beside the road who had been robbed and beaten. The first two men were religious leaders. Both of them passed by the man and ignored his needs. The third person to encounter the victim was a Samaritan, a member of an ethnic and religious group looked down upon by the Jewish religious leaders. The Samaritan stopped and helped the man, providing for his lodging and medical treatment. Jesus asked his questioner, "Which of these three was a neighbor?"

The questioner responded, "The one who showed mercy."

Jesus said, "Go and do the same" (Luke 10:29–37).

Anyone whom we have the ability to help is our neighbor. Jesus will not let us limit our neighborhood to our street or city. People in Haiti are our neighbors. People in India are our neighbors. We must have a concern for them as Jesus did.

> Father in heaven, give me the grace to love my neighbors as myself.
> Expand my understanding of my neighborhood to include anyone
> in need whom I am able to help. Amen.

Megatheme 4:
Your Heart and Your Tongue

The fourth megatheme in Proverbs is your heart and your tongue. Why are these two subjects grouped together? Proverbs says your inner life and your conversation are closely linked. The contents of your heart will spill over into your words, and your words will reveal the character of your heart. We will spend the next four weeks learning how to have a better life by cultivating a good heart and choosing good words.

Your Heart Is the Essence of Who You Are

Above all else, guard your heart,
for everything you do flows from it.
—Proverbs 4:23

As water reflects the face,
so one's life reflects the heart.
—Proverbs 27:19

Have you ever heard the saying, "You are what you eat"? That implies your body is the crux of who you are. Have you ever heard the saying, "Clothes make the man"? That implies image is central to your identity. Proverbs says your heart is the essence of who you are. In the Bible, the heart means the source of your thoughts, feelings, and will. It is your core personality, your character, your spiritual disposition. It is your inner life as contrasted to your outer activity and appearance. Proverbs says your heart is like a spring; the stream of your life flows from this source. Your heart "determines the course of your life" (Proverbs 4:23 NLT).

How's your heart? If you go to a doctor for a physical, he will probably put a stethoscope to your chest and listen to your heart. That organ in your chest is crucial to your physical health, and he wants to determine if there are any problems with your heart. It is just as important to examine your spiritual heart, your soul, the real inner you. This week, ask God to put his stethoscope to your spiritual heart and diagnose the condition of your soul.

> Lord, help me to value my inner life even more than my outer image. Teach me to measure myself and others not by external appearance but by the character of the heart. Amen.

The Character of Your Heart Is Not Obvious

The purposes of a person's heart are deep waters,
but one who has insight draws them out.
—Proverbs 20:5

Like a coating of silver dross on earthenware
are fervent lips with an evil heart.
Enemies disguise themselves with their lips,
but in their hearts they harbor deceit.
—Proverbs 26:23–24

The nature of your heart is not readily apparent. You can be very different on the outside than you are on the inside. You can disguise the character of your heart with a veneer of politeness or even religiosity. Once my wife took some silver items to a place that buys gold and silver. I went along to guard the vast profits she would make. All the items looked the same to me, but the buyer conducted a series of careful tests on them. He wanted to know what was under the outer silver coating. He proclaimed that some of them were sterling silver but others were only silver plate. The same principle applies to people: what's beneath the surface is not readily apparent.

We can even fool ourselves about the condition of our hearts. Our motives may initially be hidden even to us. We can do good things for wrong reasons. It is wise for us to look deeply into our hearts, like looking deeply into a pool of water. Pastor Chuck Swindoll said that he kept a small framed print in his office that read: "What's my motive?"

Lord, I don't want to be a hypocrite. I don't want to wear a mask that hides who I really am on the inside. I want my heart to be pure so that if you ever turn me inside out I will look even better than before. Amen.

God Looks Deeply into Your Heart

A person may think their own ways are right,
but the LORD weighs the heart.
—Proverbs 21:2

The lamp of the Lord searches the spirit of a man;
it searches out his inmost being.
—Proverbs 20:27 NIV, 1984

We tend to overrate ourselves. We think we are doing pretty well. Our ways seem right to us. We need an evaluation from an outside source. When I was in college I took a journalism class. Early in the course we were given a set of facts about a local political situation and were assigned to write a news report based on those facts. The professor asked for volunteers to read their stories to the class. I thought I had done a great job, and so I volunteered. I expected the professor to be impressed with the insight of my investigative journalism. I was a little proud. After I finished reading my story, he said gruffly, "That's not a news story. That's an editorial." I wanted to crawl under my desk, but I learned a valuable lesson about objectivity in reporting. I also learned I am not always a good judge of myself.

God is able to see within our hearts. He is very interested in our inner character, and he looks deeply into the recesses of our souls. He shines his spotlight on our hidden agendas, our secret thoughts, and motives unrecognized even by us. The wise person gives God permission to search and listens to his evaluation.

Search me, God, and know my heart; test me and know my anxious thoughts. See if there is any offensive way in me, and lead me in the way everlasting (Psalm 139:23–24). Amen.

Your Conversation Reveals Your Heart

The hearts of the wise make their mouths prudent,
and their lips promote instruction.
—Proverbs 16:23

How can you know what is in your heart? Your conversation reveals the character of your heart. Proverbs says that we can temporarily camouflage our hearts with our speech, but eventually our words will betray the nature of our hearts. In the parallel lines of several proverbs "heart" is used interchangeably with "tongue," "mouth," or "lips":

The tongue of the righteous is choice silver,
but the heart of the wicked is of little value. (Proverbs 10:20)

The lips of the wise spread knowledge,
but the hearts of fools are not upright. (Proverbs 15:7)

The heart of the righteous weighs its answers,
but the mouth of the wicked gushes evil. (Proverbs 15:28)

So one way to gauge the condition of your heart is to listen to yourself. Is your speech constantly critical? Your heart is bitter. Do you complain a lot? Your heart is not content. Is your conversation dirty or suggestive? Your heart is impure. Is your speech always trivial? Your heart is petty. We tend to excuse our profanity or criticism by saying, "That just slipped out. I didn't mean to say that." Jesus said, "The mouth speaks what the heart is full of" (Matthew 12:34).

Lord, these verses make me uncomfortable because my conversation is not always pure and positive. Help me not to shy away from this process because of its discomfort. Help me to dig deep and see the root of my comments. I want to begin to change from the inside out. Amen.

Difficult Situations Reveal Your Heart

The crucible for silver and the furnace for gold,
but the LORD tests the heart.
—Proverbs 17:3

How can you know what is in your heart? Proverbs says that difficult situations will reveal the character of your heart. In order to refine silver and gold in biblical times, ores were crushed and then heated to extremely high temperatures. The impurities would rise to the surface and could be skimmed off or blown off with a blast of air. I grew up in a copper mining town. My parents worked for a company that processed the ore. In one process, the ore was heated in blast furnaces to burn out the impurities. In another process, the ore was ground to powder and then flooded with water to float off the impurities. In the same way, God uses heat and pressure to reveal what is in our hearts and to purify them. What are you like when the heat and pressure are on? That is what your heart is like.

Reality shows illustrate this principle. In the opening episode of *Survivor* or other similar programs, everyone is polite and kind and gets along with others. Then, when hunger and fatigue set in and the competition begins, some people reveal a nasty, critical, deceptive streak. Heat and pressure have revealed their hearts. God will allow difficult situations to come into your life to reveal to you who you really are. That understanding is the first step to changing your heart.

Lord, I don't enjoy learning spiritual lessons through difficult times. But when those difficult times come, help me not to ignore the lessons they teach. I don't always like the way I act under pressure. I know you don't always like the way I act either, but I am grateful your love for me does not waver. Help me to grow through the refining process of my troubles. Amen.

God's Word Can Change Your Heart

My son, keep your father's command
and do not forsake your mother's teaching.
Bind them always on your heart;
fasten them around your neck.
—Proverbs 6:20–21

My son, keep my words
and store up my commands within you.
Keep my commands and you will live;
guard my teachings as the apple of your eye.
Bind them on your fingers;
write them on the tablet of your heart.
—Proverbs 7:1–3

What can you do to change your heart? Bind God's commandments on your heart. Etch his teachings on your heart. This means to read the Bible and meditate on what you read. Underline or copy key passages that speak to you and seek to memorize them.

Why is this important? The Word of God has a supernatural power to penetrate the deep recesses of your heart and change your hidden motives: "For the word of God is alive and active. Sharper than any double-edged sword, it penetrates even to dividing soul and spirit, joints and marrow; it judges the thoughts and attitudes of the heart" (Hebrews 4:12).

The Old Testament Law said that when a king of Israel took the throne, he was to make his own handwritten copy of the books of the Law. He was instructed to keep it with him and read it every day of his life "so that he may learn to revere the LORD his God" and "not consider himself better than his fellow Israelites" (Deuteronomy 17:19, 20). The Word of God is a powerful change agent, able to redirect your heart like few other influences.

Dear God, thank you for the gift of your Word, the Bible. Help
me to devour the Word with a spiritual hunger. Use it in my life
to change the depths of my heart. Amen.

Admit You Need God's Help
to Change Your Heart

Who can say, "I have kept my heart pure;
I am clean and without sin"?
—Proverbs 20:9

My son, give me your heart
and let your eyes delight in my ways.
—Proverbs 23:26

Your heart trouble is beyond your ability to repair. To change your heart you must admit that your heart is corrupt and that you need God's help. The Old Testament looked forward to a day when God would provide a way for us to have a heart transplant. Through the prophets, God spoke of a coming day when he would change us from the inside out: "I will give you a new heart and put a new spirit in you; I will remove from you your heart of stone and give you a heart of flesh. And I will put my Spirit in you and move you to follow my decrees and be careful to keep my laws" (Ezekiel 36:26–27). That promise is fulfilled in Jesus Christ. Jesus is a heart specialist. When you admit to him your heart trouble and trust in him, he can radically change your heart, giving you new motives and desires. He will put his Spirit within your heart, giving you new power and strength: "God's love has been poured out into our hearts through the Holy Spirit who has been given to us" (Romans 5:5).

Jesus, I acknowledge that my heart is wicked. I want a new heart!
I want a new set of desires and motivations. I ask for the gift of
your transforming Spirit. Take up residence in my heart and make
it a different place. Amen.

You Can Choose a Joyful Heart

All the days of the oppressed are wretched,
but the cheerful heart has a continual feast.
—Proverbs 15:15

Proverbs says you can choose the attitude of your heart. Even if all your days are wretched, you can have a continual feast in life if you possess a cheerful heart. Your mood does not have to be dictated by the circumstances of your life. You do not have to ride a roller coaster of emotions. You can cultivate a disposition that will enable you to have a continual feast through the ups and downs of life.

Barbara Johnson experienced more than her share of suffering in life. Her husband was on his way to a church camp when he was involved in an accident that left him blind and disabled. A son was killed in the Vietnam War. Another son was killed by a drunk driver. A third son announced he was gay and disappeared for ten years. Barbara was diagnosed with diabetes and later with central nervous system lymphoma. Throughout these tragedies she found humor in life and joy in her faith. She wrote a number of positive books including *Splashes of Joy in the Cesspools of Life* and *Pain Is Inevitable, Misery Is Optional, So Stick a Geranium in Your Hat and Be Happy.* She said, "I've learned to welcome the valleys of life because that is where we learn to do our growing. I couldn't have made it without many doses of joy and hope. Life is not always what we want, but it's what we've got. So stick a geranium in your hat and be happy."[26]

Father, help me to choose a cheerful heart. Amen.

A Joyful Heart Will Improve Your Spiritual Health

A happy heart makes the face cheerful,
but heartache crushes the spirit.
—Proverbs 15:13

The attitude of your heart is a big factor in your spiritual, emotional, and mental health. A happy heart affects the countenance of your face and your outlook on life. A sad heart crushes your spiritual well-being and can lead to depression.

Psychologists estimate that we have twenty-five thousand to fifty thousand thoughts per day. If your mind is primarily pessimistic you are generating thousands of negative thoughts each day. "One of the most powerful actions you can take in combating depression is to understand how critical the quality of your thinking is. Often you can't control how you feel, but you can always control how you think."[27] Changing negative thoughts to positive thoughts is not easy, because negative thinking becomes habitual. If you struggle with negative thoughts, try writing down every negative thought you have for a few days so you can see your behavior patterns. Ask a trusted friend to help cue you when you begin to sound negative. Try to convert negative thoughts to positive thinking. Begin to list your positive thoughts. A study published in the *American Family Physician* found that this kind of cognitive therapy combined with antidepressants can effectively manage even severe or chronic depression.[28]

> Lord God, I sometimes tend to get trapped in a cycle of negative thoughts. I ask you to help me change my habits of thinking. I want to develop new thought patterns of gratitude and joy. Amen.

A Joyful Heart Will Improve Your Physical Health

A cheerful heart is good medicine,
but a crushed spirit dries up the bones.
—Proverbs 17:22

This proverb speaks of the physical benefits of a joyful heart. A cheerful heart is "good for your health" (MSG). A crushed spirit "saps a person's strength" (NLT). A study published in the *American Journal of Cardiology* found that happy, cheerful individuals have significantly lower chances of heart attack and other cardiac problems. Researchers analyzed data on nearly fifteen hundred healthy individuals who were at high risk for coronary artery disease because of their family history. Their analysis showed that positive well-being was associated with an average 48 percent reduction in coronary artery disease in the subgroup with the highest risk. Positive well-being was described as "positive emotions like cheerfulness, a positive outlook on life, and high life satisfaction."[29] Edward Creagan writes, "Attitude creates reality. Mayo Clinic researchers have clearly documented that having a more positive, optimistic view of the situation provides health benefits for individuals with some forms of lung cancer. How you view a situation can have an enormous impact on how you live."[30]

Thanksgiving and worship are two practices that cultivate a joyful heart and create physical and spiritual benefits. Listing our blessings in personal prayer not only brings glory to God but also develops a positive attitude in our minds. Singing worship songs in church both exalts God and lifts our spirits.

Lord, I want to be physically healthy. But even more, I want to be healthy in my inner life. I ask you to heal me, beginning with the attitude of my heart. Amen.

A Joyful Heart Will Sustain You in Tough Times

A man's spirit sustains him in sickness,
but a crushed spirit who can bear?
—Proverbs 18:14 NIV, 1984

You may think this message of cultivating a joyful heart is fine for people whose lives are going well, but what about people whose lives are miserable? What about those who live with chronic pain? This is not less applicable to those who suffer; it is more applicable. A joyful heart can sustain you in sickness. A crushed spirit makes life unbearable.

Eliza Hewitt was a schoolteacher in Philadelphia in the late 1800s. One day she was attempting to correct a student who was misbehaving. He struck her across the back with a slate, causing severe injury. She was placed in a heavy cast for six months. After the cast was removed, her doctor permitted her to go for a short walk in a nearby park. It was a warm spring day, and her heart was overflowing with joy for her recovery. When she returned home she wrote the following hymn:

There is sunshine in my soul today,
More glorious and bright
Than glows in any earthly sky,
For Jesus is my light.

There is gladness in my soul today,
And hope and praise and love,
For blessings which he gives me now,
For joys "laid up" above.

O there's sunshine, blessed sunshine,
When the peaceful, happy moments roll;
When Jesus shows his smiling face,
There is sunshine in my soul.[31]

The joy within her heart sustained her in her pain and kept her from becoming a bitter person.

Father, rescue me from a victim mentality. Turn my focus to your goodness and mercy. May the sunshine of your presence fill my life today. Thank you, Lord. Amen.

Sin Robs Your Heart of Joy

Evildoers are snared by their own sin,
but the righteous shout for joy and are glad.
—Proverbs 29:6

Many people think that a self-centered life is the happiest life. We are sold the notion that sin is enjoyable. Dessert menus market rich chocolate desserts as "sinfully rich" or "decadent." Marketers have determined that we will respond to these descriptions positively rather than negatively. If we are honest, some of us think we would have more fun if we could break all God's commands as long as we did not get caught. But Proverbs says that sin cannot deliver the joy it promises. Sin can offer momentary pleasure, but it eventually ensnares its participants in pain and sorrow. On the other hand, those who follow God's way, the way of righteousness, shout for joy and are glad. So if you want to cultivate a truly joyful heart, you need to follow God's plan for your life. Are there sinful habits in your life that started because you thought they would bring you happiness? They probably haven't delivered what they promised. You can confess your sin, turn from it, and experience the joy of cleansing and forgiveness.

John Newton, who wrote the famous hymn, *Amazing Grace,* wrote another song entitled, *Glorious Things of Thee Are Spoken.* One stanza of that hymn says:

Fading is the worldling's pleasure,
All his boasted pomp and show;
Solid joys and lasting treasure
None but Zion's children know.

Father, I confess I have sometimes looked for happiness in the wrong places. Forgive me my folly. I want the solid joy and lasting treasure that only you can give. Amen.

Good News Brings Joy to the Heart

Light in a messenger's eyes brings joy to the heart,
and good news gives health to the bones.
—Proverbs 15:30

Some of the greatest times of joy in life come when we receive good news: "I got accepted to college!" "I'm getting married!" "We're having a baby!" "I got a promotion!" Ultimate joy comes from the ultimate good news: "Do not be afraid. I bring you good news that will cause great joy for all the people. Today in the town of David a Savior has been born to you; he is the Messiah, the Lord" (Luke 2:10–11). This is the message the angels announced at the birth of Jesus. The word *angel* literally means *messenger*. Angels are God's heavenly messengers. He sent them to earth to announce the best news ever: he loves us and has sent his Son, Jesus, to earth to save us from the penalty and power of our sins. That news is the source of life's greatest joy.

The night before he died, Jesus talked to his disciples about joy. He told them that complete joy could be found in a relationship with him, a relationship of love and obedience: "As my Father has loved me, so have I loved you. Now remain in my love. If you keep my commands, you will remain in my love, just as I have kept my Father's commands and remain in his love. I have told you this so that my joy may be in you and that your joy may be complete" (John 15:9–11). This good new brings joy to the heart and health to the bones.

> Dear Jesus, thank you for loving me enough to come to earth to be my Savior. I confess you as Messiah and Lord. I want to follow you today so that your joy may be in me, and my joy may be complete. Amen.

Five Steps to a More Joyful Heart

Proverb shares the benefits of a joyful heart. The New Testament tells how to cultivate a joyful heart. Here are five steps to a more joyful life:

First, review your position in Christ. "Rejoice in the Lord always" (Philippians 4:4). When you are in Christ, your sins are forgiven, and you are a child of the king. Nothing in life threatens your position in Christ. Rejoice in your identity in him.

Second, count your blessings. "Be joyful always, pray continually, give thanks in all circumstances" (1 Thessalonians 5:16–18). Be thankful for what you have instead of complaining about what you do not have.

Third, focus on your future in heaven. "We rejoice in the hope of the glory of God" (Romans 5:2 NIV, 1984). Your present circumstances may not be great, but your future will be.

Fourth, learn to share in the joy of others. "Rejoice with those who rejoice" (Romans 12:15). Connect with a church family of other believers, and you will be able to share in their joyful experiences.

Fifth, get involved in ministry to others. "Indeed, you are our glory and joy" (1 Thessalonians 2:20). Paul found his joy in sharing the gospel with others. Researcher Bernard Rimland conducted a study in which he asked participants to list the ten people they knew best and then to label them as happy or unhappy. Next, they were told to go through the same list of people and label them as selfish or unselfish. Rimland found that every single person who was labeled happy was also labeled unselfish. He wrote that those "whose activities are devoted to bringing themselves happiness ... are far less likely to be happy than those whose efforts are devoted to making others happy."[32]

> Lord Jesus, transform me by the renewing of my mind. Help me
> to think on things that are true and noble and right, things that
> are pure and lovely and admirable. Amen.

Words Have the Power of Life or Death

The tongue has the power of life and death,
and those who love it will eat its fruit.
—Proverbs 18:21

If we would be wise, Proverbs would have us be very cognizant of the power of our words. Proverbs suggests that we tend to underestimate the effect of words. Words are powerful. This is a theme throughout the Bible. God created the universe by his word (Hebrews 11:3), and the Son of God sustains all things by his word (Hebrews 1:3). Jesus is described as the eternal Word of God (John 1:1). God's plan is that by the preaching of the word people will be born again to eternal life (1 Peter 1:23–25).

This proverb says words have the power of life or death. With our words we can explain to someone how to receive the gift of eternal life, or we can destroy someone's reputation. The Message paraphrases this proverb this way: "Words kill, words give life; they're either poison or fruit—you choose."

When I was nine years old, during Vacation Bible School at my church, I listened as my pastor told us how to become followers of Jesus. He told us that Jesus loved us, that he died on the cross to pay the penalty for our sins, that he rose from the dead, and that he wanted to save and guide us. I had heard those words before. I had good parents who had spoken those words. But that day they sank into my heart, and I confessed Jesus as my Savior. That event was foundational in the direction of my life. I am thankful for those who spoke words of life to me. I am still eating the fruit of those good words.

> Lord, I sometimes don't give much thought to what I say. I underestimate the potential of my words. Give me an awareness of their power. Help me to speak words of life today. Amen.

Words Can Pierce Like a Sword or Bring Healing

The words of the reckless pierce like swords,
but the tongue of the wise brings healing.
—Proverbs 12:18

When I was a kid we tried to downplay the power of words. If a bully called someone a name, the person might respond with a rhyme: "Sticks and stones may break my bones, but names will never hurt me." Perhaps that helped to lessen the sting, but Proverbs says the opposite is true.

Words can pierce like a sword. You can probably recall right now some hurtful words that someone has said to you. You may also be able to recall some hurtful words you have spoken. Why do we do that? Proverbs says we are using our words as weapons. Sometimes we want to get back at someone, so we say something hurtful. At other times our hurtful words come from anger and bitterness entirely unrelated to the person at whom we hurl them.

Words can also bring healing. You can probably remember a time when someone brought you healing by their affirmation or encouragement.

Think of your words in terms of stewardship. Most Christians understand the concept of stewardship in regard to money. God gives us the ability to work and generate income, so we seek to manage our money in a way that honors him. The same principle applies to our words. God gives us the ability to speak, so we should manage our conversation in a way that honors him. What will you do today with the words God enables you to form on your lips? Look for ways to bring hope and healing through what you say.

> Lord, thank you for giving me the ability to speak. You formed my vocal cords and tongue and lips. I don't want to use this gift in a way that harms others. I want to be a good steward of the words you enable me to speak. Help me today to speak words that heal. Amen.

Words Can Change the Direction of a City or a Nation

Through the blessing of the upright a city is exalted,
but by the mouth of the wicked it is destroyed.
—Proverbs 11:11

The influence of words can change the direction of a city or a culture. That is why we need to pray for those who give counsel to mayors, representatives, and presidents.

This verse speaks of the power of blessing. Words of encouragement can be a powerful blessing. An exhibit at the Library of Congress displays the contents of President Lincoln's pockets the night he was shot at Ford's Theatre. In his pockets were two pairs of spectacles, a lens polisher, a handkerchief, a pocketknife, and a brown leather wallet. Inside the wallet were a Confederate five-dollar bill and eight worn newspaper clippings. Several of the newspaper clippings contained favorable comments written during the time he was running for reelection. One writer expounded, "We see in the President a brightness of personal honor on which no adversary has yet been able to fix a stain."[33] Why did Lincoln carry these clippings in his pocket? Apparently in a time when the nation was bitterly divided and his leadership was constantly criticized, he drew strength from those words of affirmation.

Perhaps you can remember the affirmation of a teacher or coach who encouraged you. Those words may have stayed with you for many years. Is there someone in your life who needs that same kind of affirmation and encouragement?

> Lord, help me to speak words of blessing that might exalt a city. Bring to my mind someone who would benefit from my affirmation. Stir me today to write or text or call someone who needs my encouragement. Amen.

Good Words Are Sweet as Honey

Gracious words are a honeycomb,
sweet to the soul and healing to the bones.
—Proverbs 16:24

I did not intend to write a book. I started writing because someone spoke gracious words to me, words that were sweet and encouraging. Several years ago I spent a year in my church preaching through the Psalms. An older woman whom I respected encouraged me to write a book based on the sermon series. I was reluctant, but she continued to encourage me. As a result I wrote my first book, *A Year in the Psalms*.[34] A few years later she died, and I missed her counsel and encouragement. Almost immediately another friend in my church, a man younger than me, began to encourage me to write another book. He continually shared what my first book had meant to him. When I spent a year preaching through Proverbs, I felt God's prompting to write again. After I started writing, this friend continually spurred me on. This writing is the result of his gracious words.

I have experienced the power of gracious words in my life. I want to speak those kinds of words to other people. I don't want to be known for my criticism or negativism. I don't want all my conversations to be about me. I want to speak words that bless other people.

Lord, help me to speak gracious words, words that are sweet to the soul and healing to the bones. Amen.

Your Words Will Bless or Curse You

The wise store up knowledge,
but the mouth of a fool invites ruin.
—Proverbs 10:14

From the fruit of their lips people are filled with good things,
and the work of their hands brings them reward.
—Proverbs 12:14

Proverbs says your words are like a boomerang. They not only impact others, but they also come back to either bless or curse you. Second Samuel 25 tells the story of a wealthy but surly man named Nabal. David and his men had protected Nabal's herdsmen in the desert. When David's men asked Nabal for supplies, he responded, "Who is this David? Who is this son of Jesse? Many servants are breaking away from their masters these days. Why should I take my bread and water, and the meat I have slaughtered for my shearers, and give it to men coming from who knows where?" David was upset and took four hundred men to attack Nabal. One of Nabal's servants told Abigail, Nabal's wife, what her husband had said. She quickly loaded provisions on donkeys and rode out to meet David. She apologized for her husband, asked David's forgiveness, thanked him for his protection, and asked for his favor when he became king. Her words diffused the situation. David said to Abigail, "May you be blessed for your good judgment and for keeping me from bloodshed this day." Ten days later the Lord struck Nabal, and he died. Later David asked Abigail to become his wife. The curses of Nabal and the blessings of Abigail returned to each of them.

> Lord, I don't want my mouth to invite ruin as did the mouth of
> Nabal. May the fruit of my lips fill people with good things as did
> the lips of Abigail. Amen.

Your Words Are a Window into Your Heart

The hearts of the wise make their mouths prudent,
and their lips promote instruction.
—Proverbs 16:23

The heart of the righteous weighs its answers,
but the mouth of the wicked gushes evil.
—Proverbs 15:28

Proverbs says there is a direct pipeline between your heart and your mouth. Your heart makes your mouth prudent. It is our tendency to deny this connection and to downplay the significance of our evil words. I like to think I am a good person who just occasionally says some unkind or hurtful things. Proverbs does not support that thinking.

Jesus said, "Everyone will have to give account on the day of judgment for every empty word they have spoken. For by your words you will be acquitted, and by your words you will be condemned" (Matthew 12:36–37). At first reading, this statement by Jesus does not seem very fair. How could it be right to judge us by our casual chitchat, by words that we speak without thinking? Jesus is affirming that the content of our hearts is accurately reflected in the conversation of our lips. Thus, our words provide a dependable assessment of the character of our souls.

Jesus, it is obvious that you take very seriously the words that I say. Help me regard them with the same earnestness. Change my heart so that my lips may not gush evil but may promote instruction. Amen.

The Most Powerful Words in the World

The message of the Bible is not, "Try harder to say the right things." The message of the Bible is that our tongues are wicked because our hearts are wicked. We are sinners. But God loves sinners and has sent us his Son to save us. Through union with Jesus you can be remade from the inside out. You can begin to become like the One whose words are just and true. Uniting with Jesus is something that occurs in your heart and in your mouth. First, you believe in your heart that Jesus is the Son of God who died and rose again. Second, you confess with your mouth that Jesus is Lord. Inner faith results in an outer confession. The most powerful words you can say are, "Jesus is Lord."

> But what does it say? "The word is near you; it is in your mouth and in your heart," that is, the message concerning faith that we proclaim: If you declare with your mouth, "Jesus is Lord," and believe in your heart that God raised him from the dead, you will be saved. For it is with your heart that you believe and are justified, and it is with your mouth that you profess your faith and are saved. (Romans 10:8–10)

This confession that Jesus is Lord is not limited to the time of conversion. We are to continue to affirm with our lips that Jesus is Lord of our lives. We make that confession in our worship when we praise Jesus as Lord. We make that confession in our witness when we share the good news of Jesus.

> Jesus, right now in prayer I utter these words that reflect the belief of my heart: You are Lord. You are Lord of the universe. You are Lord of my life. Give me courage to confess your name openly and unashamedly today. May all my words today be true to that confession. Amen.

Learn to Speak Less

The one who has knowledge uses words with restraint,
and whoever has understanding is even-tempered.
Even fools are thought wise if they keep silent,
and discerning if they hold their tongues.
—Proverbs 17:27–28

To answer before listening—
that is folly and shame.
—Proverbs 18:13

When we realize the power of our words, we will choose them carefully. Proverbs says a wise person restrains his words. Even the foolish person can be thought wise if he holds his tongue! This proverb may have been the source for Abraham Lincoln's witty saying: "It is better to keep your mouth shut and let them think you are a fool than to open your mouth and remove all doubt."[35]

Many of us simply talk too much. The University of Arizona sought to count the number of words people speak each day. They used voice-activated recorders to tally the word count for participants in their study. They found that the average person speaks sixteen thousand words each day.[36] However, there was a wide range in the data. The person with the lowest total spoke only seven hundred words, but the person with the highest total spoke forty-seven thousand words. (I know what you are thinking. You are wrong. Both the person with the lowest total and the person with the highest total were men!)

Sometimes we talk too much because we are self-absorbed. When someone else is talking, we are thinking about what we will say next and how we can top what has just been said. When we talk less, we become better listeners. We are better able to hear the voice of God through others. We are better able to be used by God to minister to others when we listen. "My dear brothers and sisters, take note of this: Everyone should be quick to listen, slow to speak and slow to become angry" (James 1:19).

Lord, I think I sometimes talk too much. Help me be quick to listen and slow to speak. When I do speak, help me to speak with intentionality and wisdom. Amen.

Learn to Filter Your Words

Those who guard their lips preserve their lives,
but those who speak rashly will come to ruin.
—Proverbs 13:3

Those who guard their mouths and their tongues
keep themselves from calamity.
—Proverbs 21:23

These proverbs tell us to guard our lips. Sometimes we speak without thinking, as if our lips are on autopilot. There needs to be a conscious gap between our thoughts and our words. Not every thought that enters our minds needs to be voiced. Proverbs says it is when we speak rashly that we come to ruin. Just as it is hard to put toothpaste back into the tube, it is hard to undo the damage of words after they are spoken.

Most heating and air conditioning systems have filters. The air that circulates through the system passes through the filter. The filter screens out dust, pollen, and other harmful particles. Think of that same concept for your mouth. Learn to filter everything that passes through your lips. Screen out comments that are hurtful or vindictive. Filter out anything that you will later regret.

Learn to filter the comments that you write in emails and that you post on social media. The internet has become a cruel place where people post hurtful comments. Perhaps the remoteness of the medium causes people to post things they would never say face-to-face.

Time is one of the best filters. I have learned the hard way that I do not need to fire off an email or make a phone call when I am angry. By waiting just a few minutes before I respond, I tend to form my thoughts into much more reasonable words.

> Lord, teach me to guard my lips. I do not want any of my words
> to bring reproach to your name or bring ruin to my life. Help me
> to filter the words I will say today. Amen.

Filter Gossip Out of Your Conversation

Proverbs has a lot to say about gossip. Proverbs acknowledges that gossip is enjoyable. It fuels our sense of self-importance to know something that someone else does not yet know. We enjoy the look on a friend's face when we tell him or her a piece of news he or she did not know. Sharing a juicy bit of gossip is like eating the middle of a cinnamon roll:

> The words of a gossip are like choice morsels;
> they go down to the inmost parts. (Proverbs 18:8)

But Proverbs warns that the enjoyment of gossip is far offset by the damage it causes. Gossip stirs up conflict and destroys friendships:

> A perverse person stirs up conflict,
> and a gossip separates close friends. (Proverbs 16:28)

Proverbs has a simple solution to the problem of gossip: don't repeat the gossip you hear:

> Without wood a fire goes out;
> without a gossip a quarrel dies down. (Proverbs 26:20)

Even if something is true, that does not mean it needs to be shared. We sometimes begin gossip with the phrase, "Don't tell anyone I told you this, but …" If you have to begin a sentence with that phrase, you probably shouldn't share it at all. Christians sometimes baptize gossip by sharing it as prayer requests. That label does not neutralize the damage it can cause.

> Dear Lord, help me find my sense of worth and importance in my relationship to you, so that I do not need to feed my ego by repeating gossip. Forgive me when I have broken the confidence someone has placed in me. May my words not be fuel for the fires of gossip. Amen.

Speak Words That Are True

Truthful lips endure forever,
but a lying tongue lasts only a moment.
—Proverbs 12:19

What a person desires is unfailing love;
Better to be poor than a liar.
—Proverbs 19:22

Buy the truth and do not sell it—
wisdom, instruction and insight as well.
—Proverbs 23:23

What kind of words does God want us to speak? Proverbs tells us to speak words that are true. Proverbs advises that if we must choose between lying and poverty, we should choose poverty. Proverbs says we should value truth more than any possession. Proverbs says truthful lips will endure, but the lying tongue lasts only a moment.

In 2 Kings 5, the Bible tells the story of a commander named Naaman who had leprosy. God healed Naaman through the ministry of his prophet Elisha. Naaman was so grateful that he wanted to give Elisha a gift, but Elisha would not accept anything. After Naaman left, Elisha's servant, Gehazi, thought, "Elisha was too easy on Naaman. I will run after him and get something from him." Gehazi found Naaman and told him, "My master sent me to say, 'Two young prophets just came to visit. Please give them a talent of silver and two sets of clothing.'" Naaman readily gave him even more than he asked. Gehazi hid the things in his house and then went to his master. Elisha asked, "Where have you been, Gehazi?"

"Your servant didn't go anywhere," he answered.

Elisha said, "Was not my spirit with you when the man got down from his chariot to meet you? Is this the time to take money or accept clothes? Naaman's leprosy will cling to you and your descendants forever."

Gehazi paid a price for his deception.

> Lord, I am sometimes tempted to lie in order to get out of trouble.
> I am tempted to flatter in order to gain an advantage. I am tempted
> to exaggerate in order to impress my friends. Let the words of these
> proverbs sink into my heart so that I will choose to speak the truth
> even when it is not easy. Amen.

Speak Words That Are Fitting

A person finds joy in giving an apt reply—
and how good is a timely word!
—Proverbs 15:23

The lips of the righteous know what is fitting,
but the mouth of the wicked only what is perverse.
—Proverbs 10:32 NIV, 1984

A word aptly spoken
is like apples of gold in settings of silver.
—Proverbs 25:11 NIV, 1984

It is not enough to speak words that are true. We must also choose words that are fitting. Some words are true, but they are not appropriate. Children often speak words that are true but are not fitting. Most parents have had the experience of being in a line at the grocery store when one of their children loudly makes an observation about the appearance of the customer in front of them. Once a child declared to a man in a wheelchair in front of me, "You are missing a leg." The statement was true; it was probably not appropriate.

On the other hand, the right word spoken at the right time can be joyous and good. It can be as beautiful as apples of gold in settings of silver. Nathaniel Hawthorne is known as the first great American novelist, but he lived in obscurity much of his life. He had a burning desire to be a writer, but for years he had written only occasionally. He worked at the Customs House in Salem, Massachusetts. One day he lost his job. Beaten and discouraged, he went home and told his wife. She responded with optimism, "Now you can write your book!" She set pen and paper before him. That afternoon he began to write *The Scarlet Letter*.[37]

Lord, I want my words today to be apt and fitting. I want them to
be like apples of gold in settings of silver. Help me to speak words
that will bring glory to you and blessing to others. Amen.

Speak Words That Are Gentle

A gentle answer turns away wrath,
but a harsh word stirs up anger.
—Proverbs 15:1

Through patience a ruler can be persuaded,
and a gentle tongue can break a bone.
—Proverbs 25:15

The real test of our language comes when someone speaks unkind or provocative words to us. Then we are tempted to slip back into old habits and "fight fire with fire." The wise learn to dampen anger rather than igniting it.

When I was a student at Southwestern Baptist Theological Seminary, I met a retired ethics professor named T. B. Maston. Dr. Maston was a living legend at Southwestern. He pioneered the work of race relations among Southern Baptists during the 1950s and 1960s. Maston had an extensive file of correspondence that came as a result of his speaking and writing on race. The letters he received were about equally divided between support and condemnation. Maston answered most of the letters. A display of his correspondence at Southwestern revealed that his answers were always polite, factual, kind, and free of condemnation, even to the most vicious letters. To a young colleague troubled by the ugly letters, Maston said, "If we are right, the Lord and time are on our side."[38]

> Lord, I sometimes tend to speak words that throw gasoline on the flames of controversy. Help me instead to trust your vindication and to speak words that quench the fires of anger. Amen.

Speak Consistently

The New Testament book that most closely resembles the book of Proverbs is the book of James. In this book of Christian wisdom, James expresses dismay that we Christians are sometimes inconsistent in the way we talk: "With the tongue we praise our Lord and Father, and with it we curse human beings, who have been made in God's likeness. Out of the same mouth come praise and cursing. My brothers and sisters, this should not be" (James 3:9–10). When I was in college I worked for a short time at a car dealership. I knew the man who owned the dealership was active in his church and served as a deacon there. I assumed he would be a good boss. The first day on the job I was disappointed to hear him regularly berate and curse his employees. James says this type of inconsistency reflects a deep character issue: "Can both fresh water and salt water flow from the same spring? My brothers and sisters, can a fig tree bear olives, or a grapevine bear figs? Neither can a salt spring produce fresh water" (James 3:11–12). If you are singing praise songs on Sunday but cursing or gossiping on Monday, James suggests that you need to examine who you really are. At best, your inconsistency suggests a need for deep repentance. At worst, it suggests you may be deceiving yourself about your relationship with God. Your words are a barometer of the condition of your heart. A transformed heart manifests itself in language that begins to sound more and more like Jesus.

> May the words of my mouth and the meditation of my heart be pleasing in your sight, O LORD, my Rock and my Redeemer (Psalm 19:14).

Megatheme 5:
Your Money and Your Future

The final megatheme in Proverbs deals with the money you make and the plans you make. We will learn that the wise person is a shrewd manager of his money and his time. We will also learn that the wise person recognizes he is not in complete control of either of these areas, so he submits to the sovereignty of God. These proverbs contain a wealth of simple, practical wisdom. Many people experience needless pain because they ignore God's principles in these two areas. When we follow God's direction, we reap great dividends. We will invest the next five weeks absorbing God's wisdom about money and the future.

Make Your Money Honestly

God cares about how you acquire your money. God wants you to acquire your money by honest means:

> Food gained by fraud tastes sweet,
> but one ends up with a mouth full of gravel. (Proverbs 20:17)

The word *fraud* is also translated *deceit* (NKJV) and *stealing* (NLT). If you are shoplifting or stealing from your employer, God is not pleased with you. If you are cheating your customers or failing to deliver what you promised in your business, God is not pleased with you. If you are involved in a sophisticated scheme to defraud companies or investors, God is not pleased, and you will not be blessed.

This proverb contains the principle that you will reap what you sow. It acknowledges that fraud or deceit can bring short-term gains: "Food gained by fraud tastes sweet." It asserts that these acts will not bring long-term reward: "But one ends up with a mouth full of gravel."

> A fortune made by a lying tongue
> is a fleeting vapor and a deadly snare. (Proverbs 21:6)

This proverb warns of two dangers to money made by deceit. You will often lose that money (a fleeting vapor). Worse than that, you do spiritual damage to your soul (a deadly snare). Deceit in one area of life hardens your soul to deceit in other relationships.

> Dear God, I want your blessing on my work. I know that you will not bless dishonesty. I know that I tend to rationalize my behavior. Help me to see if any of my business practices, work habits, or accounting procedures are fraudulent. I want to repent and turn from those practices. I want to honor you. Amen.

Avoid Get-Rich-Quick Schemes

An inheritance quickly gained at the beginning
will not be blessed at the end.
—Proverbs 20:21 NIV, 1984

Proverbs warns about money quickly gained. If you receive some large inheritance or windfall profit, there is nothing wrong with taking it, but that should not be your approach to acquiring money. If a proposal or investment seems too good to be true, it probably is. Many people have lost their life savings in pyramid schemes and other fraudulent investments.

This proverb also applies to gambling. Americans have become obsessed with Powerball and other lotteries in the last few decades. Forty-three of the fifty states now have legal lotteries. The average American household loses almost $600 each year in the lottery. Poor people (those with incomes under $13,000) spend 9 percent of their income on the lottery.[39] Including all forms of legal gambling, the average household wagers over $1,000 each year in hopes of getting rich quickly.

By contrast, God says to plan on making money little by little:

> Dishonest money dwindles away,
> but whoever gathers money little by little makes it grow. (Proverbs 13:11)

Most of us started with a first job that paid very little money. In my first job in high school, I made $1.25 per hour. (Granted, that was in the age of the dinosaurs, but still you couldn't get a good brontosaurus burger for $1.25). When we gather money little by little, it teaches us the value of money and the importance of wise management. We are then better prepared to be stewards of a larger income. That is part of God's plan for us.

> Heavenly Father, help me to control my greed. Enable me to resist the schemes that would promise me instant riches. Help me instead to trust you to meet my needs. Amen.

Work Hard

Those who work their land will have abundant food,
but those who chase fantasies will have their fill of poverty.
—Proverbs 28:19

God's plan for acquiring money is to work. We are losing our work ethic in America. We are creating a culture of entitlement in which we think we deserve free health care, a free college education, and even free cell phones. A 2013 study by the Cato Institute reported that welfare pays more than minimum wage in thirty-five states. Welfare pays more than the average salary of a first-year teacher in eleven states.[40] Roughly 50 percent of our national budget goes to entitlement programs.

In this prevailing climate, it is important for parents to teach their children to work. Younger children need chores assigned to them. They need to learn that every member of the household has work to do. Older children and teens need to have the opportunity to do additional work to earn money for purchases they want to make.

Certainly, there are those who are unable to work. We will see that Proverbs has a lot to say about compassion as well. We must gladly provide for those who cannot work. That is why it is even more important that those who are able become productive workers in society.

> Lord, thank you for the ability you have given me to work. Help me find pleasure in honest work and satisfaction in a job well done. Amen.

Don't Be a Sluggard

In Proverbs the word for a lazy person is *sluggard*. Are you a sluggard? How do you know? The following proverb describes seven characteristics of a sluggard. Apply this checklist to yourself, your employees, or to the twenty-eight-year-old living in your basement.

1.   The sluggard is not a self-starter. He requires constant supervision:

Go to the ant, you sluggard; consider its ways and be wise!
It has no commander, no overseer or ruler,
yet it stores its provisions in summer
and gathers its food at harvest. (Proverbs 6:6–8)

2.   The sluggard is in constant conflict with his supervisors:

As vinegar to the teeth and smoke to the eyes,
so are sluggards to those who send them. (Proverbs 10:26)

3.   The sluggard does not plan for the future. He does not think beyond the present:

Sluggards do not plow in season;
so a harvest time they look but find nothing. (Proverbs 20:4)

4.   The sluggard always has an excuse for his lack of productivity:

The sluggard says, "There's a lion outside!
I'll be killed in the public square!" (Proverbs 22:13)

5.   The sluggard loves to sleep:

As a door turns on its hinges,
so a sluggard turns on his bed. (Proverbs 26:14)

6.   The sluggard does not finish what he starts:

A sluggard buries his hand in the dish;
he is too lazy to bring it back to his mouth. (Proverbs 26:15)

7.   The sluggard is a know-it-all. He is not teachable:

A sluggard is wiser in his own eyes
than seven people who answer discreetly. (Proverbs 26:16)

How did you do on the sluggard checklist? A score of 1–2 may indicate a normal person. A score of 3–4 indicates there is a problem. A score of 5 or more says it is time to throw that bum out of your house!

Lord, forgive the sin of laziness in my life. Forgive me if I have
enabled others to follow that path. Amen.

Take Care of Your Possessions

The lazy man does not roast his game,
but the diligent man prizes his possessions.
—Proverbs 12:27 NIV, 1984

It is too much trouble for a lazy person to cook the game he hunts; he just eats it raw! The opposite of a sluggard in Proverbs is a diligent person. The root of the Hebrew word translated *diligent* means "to cut" or "to decide." It means to be sharp, alert, watching for opportunities, and decisive. How do you recognize a diligent person? Proverbs says the diligent person takes care of his possessions. In the context of this verse, that means he carefully cleans, prepares, and preserves the game he kills. He does not waste the meat. In our context, the diligent person is one who values what God has given him and does not waste God's resources. A diligent person conserves energy and recycles. A diligent person donates unwanted items to Goodwill or other charities. A diligent person takes care of his home, his car, and the other possessions God has entrusted to him. These may seem like inconsequential matters. The Bible views little responsibilities as a proving ground for greater stewardship opportunities. Jesus said, "Whoever can be trusted with very little can also be trusted with much" (Luke 16:10).

> Lord, forgive me if I have been a poor steward of the possessions
> and resources you have given to me. I want to manage everything
> I have for your glory. Amen.

Do Not Wear Yourself Out Trying to Get Rich

Do not wear yourself out to get rich;
do not trust your own cleverness.
—Proverbs 23:4

When it comes to work, the sluggard is one extreme and the workaholic is the other. The devil will try to tempt you in different directions according to your makeup. He is just as content to push you into becoming a greedy person as a lazy person. We have a problem with sluggards in America. We also have a problem with workaholics and those who are consumed with riches. Proverbs says to exercise restraint. God built a Sabbath into his plan. God intends for you to have some margins in your life. These margins enable you to worship. They remind you that some things are more important than wealth:

Wealth is worthless in the day of wrath,
but righteousness delivers from death. (Proverbs 11:4)

The all-consuming pursuit of riches makes one short-sighted. To counteract greed, consider your death, the moment when you will surrender all your investments and possessions. An eternal perspective will restore to you a sense of value. On Judgment Day money will be worthless, but righteousness will be invaluable.

O Lord, you are the Maker of heaven and earth. After you made everything, you rested on the seventh day. Enable me to be like you. Give me the rhythms of work and rest that you have modeled. Amen.

Jesus Can Give Meaning to Any Work

What does the New Testament say about acquiring money? It reaffirms the principles found in Proverbs, and it offers the power to transform your work ethic. If you are a thief or a sluggard, the New Testament calls you to change: "Anyone who has been stealing must steal no longer, but must work, doing something useful with their own hands, that they may have something to share with those in need" (Ephesians 4:28). If you are a shoplifter or if you are involved in an elaborate kickback scheme, Jesus calls you to repentance. He will forgive your sin and set you on a new course in life.

Jesus can give meaning and purpose to your work no matter how menial it seems: "Whatever you do, work at it with all your heart, as working for the Lord, not for human masters, since you know that you will receive an inheritance from the Lord as a reward. It is Christ you are serving" (Colossians 3:23–24). These words were originally written to slaves. Even a servant can do his work for the Lord. Many people are not content with their jobs and want to find another one. If you can get a better job, by all means do so. But God has a purpose for you in your present job while you are there. You can find joy and contentment in any job when you realize you are working for Jesus. Whether you are bagging groceries, pumping septic tanks, or managing an investment fund, you can do your work for the glory of God.

> Lord Jesus, I lift up my work as an offering to you. I want it to be pleasing to you. Fill my days with meaning as I seek to serve you in every workday. Help me see your purposes for me in my workplace. Amen.

Give God the First Tenth of Your Income

Proverbs not only tells us how to make money wisely but also how to spend money wisely. This week we will learn five principles about what to do with our money. First, Proverbs says to give God the first portion of your income:

> Honor the Lord with your wealth,
> with the firstfruits of all your crops;
> then your barns will be filled to overflowing,
> and your vats will brim over with new wine. (Proverbs 3:9–10)

The principle of firstfruits was established in the Old Testament law. The Israelites were to give to God the first sheaf of grain from the barley and wheat harvest, the first offspring of each goat or sheep, and the first shearing of the wool. This reminded them that God was the source of all their blessings. Giving the first of your income to God establishes what is first in your life. It is an act of worship. So here is the first thing to do with your money. Every pay period make your first transaction a gift to God through his church.

How much should you give? The law prescribed that the tithe—the first 10 percent of your income—belonged to God: "A tithe of everything from the land, whether grain from the soil or fruit from the trees, belongs to the LORD; it is holy to the LORD" (Leviticus 27:30). Tithing is still a good beginning guideline for Christians.

Proverbs emphasizes that giving to God first is not only the right thing to do, but that it brings you blessing. I counsel even those in financial trouble to begin to tithe immediately, because the attitude it will create in you is even more important than the mathematics of your debt.

> Lord, I want to give you first place in all my life, including my finances. I am grateful for all you have given me. I commit myself to give back to you at least 10 percent of my income in gratitude and worship. Lord, this goes against my natural inclination to clutch my money and spend it on myself. I trust you to provide for me as I put you first in my life. Amen.

Save for the Future

The wise store up choice food and olive oil,
but fools gulp theirs down.
—Proverbs 21:20

The second element in a good money management plan is to save for the future. The wise person does not spend everything he earns. The fool gulps down everything, but the wise person has savings. He develops an emergency fund. Financial planners recommend that the first step in a savings plan is to get $1,000 in the bank as soon as possible. Most Americans do not have an emergency fund of $1,000.[41] If you are in debt, make the minimum payments on your debts until you fund your savings account to this level. This will be your cushion against life's inevitable calamities. When you have to spend from your emergency fund, immediately set out to replenish it. Your savings second goal is to save an amount equal to three months of living expenses. This is your cushion in case you are sick, or you lose your job. After you have accomplished this, you can begin to save for other specific goals, such as a car, college, or a house.

A good financial plan is to give God 10 percent of your income, pay yourself 10 percent in a savings account, and live on 80 percent. Start these two habits of tithing and saving as early in life as possible. Start it with your part-time jobs as a teenager. Parents, teach your kids these two wise principles. I recommend giving children an allowance by the time they are in first grade. Give them their allowance in units of ten (ten dimes, ten quarters, or ten dollars, depending on their age). Teach them to give one unit to God and to save one unit in a piggy bank. Allow them to spend the rest.

Lord, help me be wise with the money you have entrusted to me.
Give me the discipline I need to save for the future. Amen.

Does Jesus Want Me to Save or Give It All Away?

The wise store up choice food and olive oil,
but fools gulp theirs down.
—Proverbs 21:20

When Jesus heard this, he said to him, "You still lack one thing.
Sell everything you have and give to the poor, and you will have treasure in heaven.
Then come, follow me.
—Luke 18:22

Proverbs tells us to save for the future. Jesus told the rich young ruler to sell all he had and give to the poor. Which are we supposed to do? Is there a contradiction in these two Bible passages? No. Proverbs provides the general principle of wise money management. This is the default plan where all of us should start. Jesus's command was directed to a particular person; he did not call everyone to do this. When we follow Christ, he is Lord of everything. He may call you to give away your possessions. If so, obey him in faith. Sound financial management is not at odds with radical obedience. Rather it provides the foundation from which you can readily respond to the Lord's call. God may call you to quit your job and move to a different city to help start a new church. If so, you will be in a much better position to answer that call if you have been following the money management advice of Proverbs. God may call you to help a fellow church member who is in financial trouble. You will have the capacity to obey him if you have been disciplined in saving money each month.

Jesus, you are Lord of everything I have including my money. I put my resources at your disposal. I want to honor you by being both wise and obedient. Give me discernment as I invest my resources in your kingdom. Amen.

Avoid Debt

The rich rule over the poor,
and the borrower is slave to the lender.
—Proverbs 22:7

The third element in a good money management plan is to avoid debt as much as possible. Proverbs says that debt is enslaving. Does this mean that it is always sinful to borrow money? No, I don't think so. Proverbs is reminding us that debt is a serious, binding commitment that should be approached cautiously. In our culture, most people have to borrow money in order to buy a home. If you try to save until you have enough cash to buy a home, rising home prices may outstrip your savings rate so that you are never able to purchase a home. While some people have gotten into financial trouble by borrowing for a home (by having too small a down payment or buying a home they could not afford), the greater problem in our culture is consumer debt or credit card debt. We go into debt for luxuries or for daily expenses for which we should pay cash. A big part of our problem is that we have not learned to be content with what we have. Proverbs warns about the danger of being enamored with the luxuries of life:

Whoever loves pleasure will become poor;
whoever loves wine and olive oil will never be rich. (Proverbs 21:17)

If you have already accumulated consumer debt, you need to work aggressively to pay it off. First, stop the bleeding. Stop spending more than you make. Identify the sources of temptation for you. You may have to cut up your credit cards. You may have to stop eating out or stop wearing brand name clothes (gasp!). Second, devote every extra dollar to extra payments on your loan balances.

Lord, I recognize the root problem in my money management is
my covetous desire for more. Please help me to exercise self-control
and to be content with the good things you have given me. Amen.

Develop a Budget

The plans of the diligent lead to profit
as surely as haste leads to poverty.
—Proverbs 21:5

The fourth element in a good money management plan is to develop a budget and to live within that budget. Plan where every dollar of your paycheck will go before you spend the first dollar. List on paper or on a spreadsheet all of your expenses, your debt payments, your savings, and your giving. You may have a line item for "mad money" or "discretionary spending," but make sure every dollar is in a category. Do not make a budget based on what you hope your future income will be next month. Be realistic and construct your budget based on the paycheck you have in your hand or on last month's income. If your expenses total more than your income, you have two choices: you must either decrease your expenses or increase your income. The most immediate choice is to cut your expenses. For most Americans, dining out, entertainment, and technology are the areas where the first cuts need to be made. If your budget is drastically out of balance, you must change the big expenses: selling your car to eliminate your car payment and buying a cheaper vehicle or downsizing your house.

If you are married, you will need to go through this process with your spouse. Money can be one of the greatest stress factors in a marriage, but it can also be a great unifying factor as you learn to compromise together, make sacrifices together, and set financial goals together.

Lord, I commit myself to live on a budget. I need your help as I
exercise discipline and create new habits in my life. Thank you,
Lord, for your involvement in the details of my life. Amen.

Be Generous

One person gives freely, yet gains even more;
another withholds unduly, but comes to poverty.
A generous person will prosper;
whoever refreshes others will be refreshed.
—Proverbs 11:24–25

The fifth element in a good money management plan is generosity. The rationale for us to save and to budget and to exercise restraint is not so that we will be filthy rich and have piles of money. The purpose of wise money management is so that we can build his kingdom and help others. Proverbs promotes generosity as a way of life beyond the tithe.

Proverbs emphasizes that generosity not only helps others but blesses you. In God's economy, when you give freely, you gain even more. He who refreshes others will be refreshed. God channels his resources to those who will use them to bless others. Jesus said the same thing: "Give, and it will be given to you. A good measure, pressed down, shaken together and running over, will be poured into your lap. For with the measure you use, it will be measured to you" (Luke 6:38).

As you follow the advice of Proverbs, you will find yourself with a better financial foundation. You will gain control of spending, eliminate debt, and develop savings. God is positioning you to become a channel of blessing. Look for needs that you can meet.

Father, as I focus on getting my finances in order, do not let me
fall into self-centeredness. Open my eyes to where you want me
to invest your resources. Amen.

You Will Give an Account of How You Spend Your Money

The New Testament continues the emphasis of Proverbs on the importance of how we spend our money. Once Jesus told a story about a man who was going away on a long trip. Before he left he distributed some of his funds to his servants for investment. He gave them different amounts based on his assessment of their management skills. He gave one servant five bags of gold. He gave two bags of gold to a second servant. He entrusted a third servant with one bag of gold. Then he went away on his trip. The first two servants worked hard to invest the money they had received, but the third servant did nothing with the funds entrusted to him. After a long time, the man returned and reviewed his accounts. The first two servants had both doubled their master's investment. The third servant presented to his master the same amount he had been given. The master praised the first two servants. He rewarded them and promoted them, giving them even more authority. The master chastised the lazy servant and dismissed him. He took the funds he had entrusted to this servant and divided them among the accounts of the first two (Matthew 25:14–29).

Jesus has given us all some stuff to manage. He has given different people different amounts. That is his prerogative. He has gone away. We are to be wise stewards of his resources. We are to use his stuff to help people and to build his kingdom. Jesus is coming back. When he gets back he is going to ask us what we have done with the stuff he gave us to manage. There will be great commendation for those who have spent his resources in a way that pleases him.

> Lord Jesus, I want to be a good manager of the things you have entrusted to me. So, give me an eternal, kingdom-centered view of my spending. Amen.

Some Poverty Comes from Laziness

The wise person does not focus totally on himself or his own prosperity. The wise person helps the poor. Proverbs has a lot to say about poverty and the poor. At least forty-three proverbs mention this subject. Proverbs has a two-sided approach to poverty, and so should we.

On the one hand Proverbs says that some poverty comes from laziness:

> Lazy hands make for poverty,
> but diligent hands bring wealth. (Proverbs 10:4)

Proverbs has a negative view of those who will not work:

> All hard work brings a profit,
> but mere talk leads only to poverty. (Proverbs 14:23)

The New Testament echoes this disdain for those who experience poverty because of their unwillingness to work:

> For even when we were with you, we gave you this rule: "The one who is unwilling to work shall not eat." We hear that some among you are idle and disruptive. They are not busy; they are busybodies. Such people we command and urge in the Lord Jesus Christ to settle down and earn the food they eat. (2 Thessalonians 3:10–12)

God does not want us to facilitate poverty that comes from laziness. He does not want us to enable the poor who will not work. This presents a challenge to Christians and to churches who want to help alleviate poverty in a way that does not create dependency.

> Lord, I pray for leaders in government, in business, and in my church as they seek to help the poor. Give them wisdom and discernment as they create systems to help the needy. Enable me to be both compassionate and judicious in my charity. Amen.

Some Poverty Comes from Injustice

Proverbs will not allow us to blame all poverty on laziness. Proverbs says most people in poverty are there because of circumstances beyond their control. Proverbs says injustice creates much of the poverty of the world:

> An unplowed field produces food for the poor,
> but injustice sweeps it away. (Proverbs 13:23)

In our business dealings we must be careful not to abuse the poor because they lack power or leverage. In our court systems we must take care that the poor are not oppressed because they lack the resources to defend themselves. God says he will serve as a defense attorney for the poor:

> Do not exploit the poor because they are poor
> and do not crush the needy in court,
> for the LORD will take up their case
> and will exact life for life. (Proverbs 22:22–23)

> Do not move an ancient boundary stone
> or encroach on the fields of the fatherless,
> for their Defender is strong;
> he will take up their case against you. (Proverbs 23:10–11)

The word *Defender* in this proverb is the same word as *guardian-redeemer* in the story of Ruth and Boaz. Boaz protected and provided for Ruth as her defender. God will act in that same way for the poor.

> Lord, I pray for justice in our nation. I pray for fairness in our court systems. I pray that you will help me examine my life and my business dealings. Show me if I have taken advantage of anyone or mistreated anyone because of their economic or social standing. Forgive me, and help me to be a defender of the poor as you are. Amen.

Realize What You Have in Common with the Poor

Rich and poor have this in common:
the LORD is the Maker of them all.
—Proverbs 22:2

Many of us in America tend to think of different groups of people in terms of *us* and *them*. We have an unspoken pride in the fact that *we* are not like *them*. We tend to think if *they* worked as hard as *we* do, *they* would not be in the shape *they* are in. Proverbs does not allow us to put too much separation between ourselves and the poor. Proverbs emphasizes a commonality that disarms our haughty spirit. A key word in Proverbs in relation to the poor is *Maker*. God is their Maker just as he is our Maker. God has given us what we have. If we had been born in a different family or a different nation, *we* might be just like *them*.

Another wisdom book in the Old Testament tells the story of Job. Job was a very rich man. In one day, in a series of natural disasters and enemy attacks, Job lost all his riches. He became poor. Job was able to keep some perspective in his devastating loss, for he realized that God had given him all he possessed. He said, "Naked I came from my mother's womb, and naked I will depart. The LORD gave and the LORD has taken away. May the name of the LORD be praised" (Job 1:21). When all our clothes and bank accounts are stripped away, we are all the same before the Lord.

Lord, you are the Maker of everything and everyone. Forgive me
if I have considered myself better than other people made in your
image. Help me to see value and worth in every person I meet
today. Amen.

Do Not Mock the Poor

Whoever mocks the poor shows contempt for their Maker;
whoever gloats over disaster will not go unpunished.
—Proverbs 17:5

Have you ever made fun of someone for their out-of-style clothes? Have you ever laughed with your friends at someone's bad haircut or clunker of a car? Proverbs says when you show contempt for the poor you are showing contempt for the One who made them, for they are his handiwork. If you do not understand this principle, try this exercise. When you see the artwork of a friend's child displayed on the family's refrigerator, say to them: "That is the worst drawing I have ever seen. The coloring is sloppy. The subject matter is unrecognizable. I would be ashamed to have that on my refrigerator." I predict that parent will not be happy with your comments. We are naturally defensive regarding our handiwork and that of those we love. So is God. He is the Maker of the poor.

Why did God make the poor? God created the poor to teach us humility. More followers of Christ come from the ranks of the poor than from the rich:

Brothers and sisters, think of what you were when you were called. Not many of you were wise by human standards; not many were influential; not many were of noble birth. God chose the foolish things of the world to shame the wise; God chose the weak things of the world to shame the strong. God chose the lowly things of this world and the despised things—and the things that are not— to nullify the things that are, so that no one may boast before him. (1 Corinthians 1:27–29)

Listen, my dear brothers and sisters: Has not God chosen those who are poor in the eyes of the world to be rich in faith and to inherit the kingdom he promised those who love him? But you have dishonored the poor. (James 1:5–6)

Father, I now see that my disparaging comments about the poor are an insult to you. I ask your forgiveness. Change my thinking and my conversation concerning the poor. Amen.

Do Not Ignore the Needs of the Poor

Whoever shuts their ears to the cry of the poor
will also cry out and not be answered.
—Proverbs 21:13

Those of us who enjoy the affluence of America are often insulated from the terrible poverty of much of the world. We can live our lives without ever thinking about the billions of people in the world who live without clean water or sewer systems. We do not know any of the one billion people in our world who live on less than one dollar a day. We do not encounter any of the sixteen thousand children who die every day from hunger-related causes. While we spend about $500 per household each year on pet food and pet supplies, we do not make much connection between our luxury and the world's poverty.

Proverbs calls us to open our ears and listen to the cries of the poor. We must become aware of the needs of our fellow human beings. We must learn of their plight even when it makes us uncomfortable. We cannot use politics or logistics or corruption as excuses for our failure to respond to world hunger. This proverb says compassion for the poor is vital to our own relationship to God. The person who ignores the needs of the poor may not be aware of his own spiritual poverty before God.

> Lord, thank you that you are always attentive to my prayers for help. Enable me to listen to the needs of the poor with that same godlike sensitivity. Amen.

Be Kind to the Poor

It is a sin to despise one's neighbor,
but blessed is the one who is kind to the needy.
—Proverbs 14:21

Whoever oppresses the poor shows contempt for their Maker,
but whoever is kind to the needy honors God.
—Proverbs 14:31

A few years ago I became convicted about my lack of personal involvement with the poor of the world. I tithed through my church and contributed to local food drives, but I felt I should share some of my abundance with the poorest of the world. Like many Christians, I was not sure what to do. How could I make a difference? I knew that much world poverty was systemic—fueled by oppressive governments, corrupt officials, and organized crime. Then I read a cover story in *Christianity Today* entitled "Want to Change the World? Sponsor a Child."[42] It told of a University of San Francisco economist who studied ten thousand children in six countries who had been sponsored twenty to thirty years ago. He found that sponsored children grew up to be adults with remarkable increases in education, jobs, and standard of living. My wife and I began to sponsor a child through Compassion International. For thirty-eight dollars a month (about the price of a nice dinner in America), the child would receive nutrition, tutoring, books, and other benefits. We liked that the money was administered by a local church or ministry center that shared the Good News of Jesus.

> Lord, I am tempted to become cynical and discouraged by all the corruption and fraud in the world. Sometimes I use these feelings as an excuse not to be kind to the poor. Forgive me for my rationalizations. Help me to hear your word in Proverbs today. Guide me to know how to obey these verses. Amen.

Good Will Repay Our Kindness to the Poor

Whoever is kind to the poor lends to the LORD,
and he will reward them for what they have done.
—Proverbs 19:17

God considers our gifts to the poor as a loan to him. Do you think God would be a good loan risk? I do! I think God will keep his word and pay back his loans with a good return on investment.

The New Testament continues this theme. Once Jesus was a dinner guest. He said to his host:

> When you give a luncheon or dinner, do not invite your friends, your brothers or sisters, your relatives, or your rich neighbors; if you do, they may invite you back and so you will be repaid. But when you give a banquet, invite the poor, the crippled, the lame, the blind, and you will be blessed. Although they cannot repay you, you will be repaid at the resurrection of the righteous. (Luke 14:12–14)

In both these passages, God is calling us to examine our investment strategy. He is calling us to rebalance our portfolios and shift more of our wealth to long-term investments. He is calling us to forgo short-term gains and consider investments that produce eternal benefits. The savvy investor will put his assets in funds that pay benefits forever. This is certainly not the only reason for helping the poor, but God says it is a legitimate source of motivation for our kindness.

Lord, make me a wise investor of my resources. Give me the faith to invest in eternity by giving to the poor. Amen.

It Is Wise to Plan Ahead

The wisdom of the prudent is to give thought to their ways,
but the folly of fools is deception.
—Proverbs 14:8

The simple believe anything,
but the prudent give thought to their steps.
—Proverbs 14:15

Are you giving any thought to where you are headed in life? Proverbs says that wisdom makes a person prudent and that prudence is characterized by giving thought to your direction in life. Many people do not give much thought to where their lives are headed; they just live day to day and week to week. The problem with that approach is that every life is headed somewhere. Like a canoe on a stream, if we do not guide our lives we will drift in some direction. These two proverbs tell us that a rudderless life is likely to drift into deception and gullibility. That is, if you don't have a plan for your life, someone else will.

This week give some thought to the trajectory of your life. First, look back at where you have been. Where were you five years ago? Think about your relationships, finances, education, and career. Most importantly, give thought to your spiritual life. Are you closer to God, deeper in your faith, and more involved in his kingdom now than you were five years ago? Or have you drifted? Second, look ahead. Where do you want to be five years from now? How do you want your life to be different? Motivational speaker Zig Ziglar often said, "Aim at nothing, and you will hit it every time."

> Lord, I am often preoccupied with the day-to-day tasks of life. I do not give enough thought to where my life is going. This week help me to look ahead. Help me be prudent enough to give thought to my ways and to make plans that will bless me and honor you. Amen.

What Is Your Goal in Life?

The plans of the diligent lead to profit
as surely as haste leads to poverty.
—Proverbs 21:5

A wicked man puts up a bold front,
but the upright give thought to their ways.
—Proverbs 21:29

Before you can make plans, you need to set some goals. A goal describes where you want to go. A plan is a strategy for how you will achieve that goal. Do you have a life goal, a statement of what you want your life to be? Do you have any clearly defined spiritual goals? What if you gave the same energy to the goals for your soul that you give to your career or financial goals?

Jonathan Edwards was a young man who lived in the early 1700s. Like many Christian teenagers, he had diverse interests and was not sure of the direction of his life. In 1722, when he was eighteen years old, he was called to pastor a group that had split from a Presbyterian church in New York City. Over the next year he wrote seventy resolutions that would govern his life. The first of these resolutions sounds like a life goal: "Resolved, that I will do whatever I think to be most to God's glory and my own good, profit and pleasure, in the whole of my duration." Some goals dealt with time management, others with prayer, Bible study, and confession of sin. Edwards determined that he would review his list every week for the rest of his life. He went on to become one of the most influential people in American history. His preaching and writing helped spawn the Great Awakening, a revival that formed the soul of colonial America. His writing is still studied in college literature classes. He became president of Princeton. He is an example of a young man who does not just put up a bold front but gives careful thought to his ways.

> Lord, help me define and articulate my life purpose, the overarching goal for my existence. Help me not to rush through this task, for your Word says that haste leads to poverty. May this statement not just be a bold front but a true reflection of the aim of my heart. Amen.

Make Plans That Are Good

Do not those who plot evil go astray?
But those who plan what is good find love and faithfulness.
—Proverbs 14:22

Many of us are consumed with self-centered plans rather than God-centered plans. The term "bucket list" has become widespread in American culture in the last twenty years. It comes from the phrase "kicking the bucket" (meaning "to die"), and it indicates a list of things one wishes to experience before death. It was popularized by the 2007 movie *The Bucket List* which starred Jack Nicholson and Morgan Freeman as terminal cancer patients. A bucket list can be a good thing; it is wise to set goals. The problem is that most versions of the bucket list in American culture are centered on exotic experiences of travel or pleasure. Ask your friends about their bucket lists or survey bucket lists on the internet, and you will hear items such as skydiving, running with the bulls, or seeing the pyramids. It is rarer to hear on someone's bucket list items such as reading the Bible through, working in a homeless shelter, or teaching English as a second language. Our problem is not that we are failing to dream; our problem is that our dreams are too small, too shallow, and too self-centered. Proverbs challenges us to plan what is good, and thereby find love and faithfulness.

Lord, are my plans good? I want to center all my life, including my plans, around your kingdom purposes. Stretch my dreams and deepen my plans. Amen.

Seek Advice from Wise People

Plans are established by seeking advice;
so if you wage war, obtain guidance.
—Proverbs 20:18

Often when we become enthusiastic about our plans, we fail to recognize pitfalls and costs. We focus only on the positive aspects of our plans and ignore the negative. We certainly don't want anyone raining on our parade. Sometime we fail to ask advice because we are too proud to ask for help. Other times we shun advice because deep down we know there are some risks with our plan, and we don't want to consider them.

Proverbs says the wise person is teachable. He is humble enough to recognize that he does not know everything. He seeks out the counsel of wise people in his church, and he listens to the voice of the Holy Spirit speaking through them. He gives consideration to negative assessments that he does not really want to hear.

There are times when the Christian must go against the prevailing counsel of his peers. When Martin Luther set forth the principles of the Reformation, he was commanded by the church of his day to recant. He was convinced he was following scripture, so he responded, "Here I stand; I can do no other." When William Carey rose to make a case for international missions, he was told by some fellow pastors to sit down and be quiet. He could not do so. Human counsel is not infallible; only the Word of God is. But when Christians ignore the counsel of their peers, it should only be after careful listening and humble reflection.

Lord, bring to my mind wise people who could be a resource to me
in the plans for my life. Give me the humility to ask their advice
and the wisdom to really listen to what they say. Amen.

Pray about Your Plans

Commit to the LORD whatever you do,
and he will establish your plans.
—Proverbs 16:3 ·

Several years ago I preached a sermon on the story of Jesus giving sight to a blind man named Bartimaeus (Mark 10:46–52). Bartimaeus was calling out to Jesus as he walked on the road to Jericho. Jesus stopped and talked to him. I was struck by Jesus's question to Bartimaeus: "What do you want me to do for you?" Jesus gave him the opportunity to exercise his faith. Bartimaeus could have asked for something small such as money. He said, "Rabbi, I want to see." Jesus healed him. I preached a sermon entitled "What Do You Want Jesus to Do for You?" I suggested that Jesus invites us to exercise faith and that we ought to tell Jesus what we want him to do in our lives. I decided I should put my preaching into practice in my own life. So that week I made a list of what I wanted Jesus to do in my life, in my family, and in my church. This was a list of my overarching dreams and desires and plans. It was a list I believed would honor God. Some of the things on my list seemed impossible at the time. At the conclusion of that sermon on Sunday, my wife and I knelt at the front of the church and presented our list to God. That was twelve years ago. I have kept that list in my prayer notebook through these years. Today I hold that same list in my hand, and I am amazed that God has brought most of those desires and plans to fruition. He has acted beyond my dreams.

Lord, I lay my plans before you. I commit them to you. I want them to honor you and advance your kingdom. I ask you to establish my plans according to your will. Amen.

Your Path Is More Important than Your Plans

The path of life leads upward for the prudent
to keep them from going down to the realm of the dead.
—Proverbs 15:24

Listen, my son, and be wise,
and set your heart on the right path.
—Proverbs 23:19

In the way of righteousness there is life;
along that path is immortality.
—Proverbs 12:28

So far this week we have learned that it is foolish to live with no thought for the future. It is important to plan ahead. However, Proverbs indicates our *path* is even more important than our *plans*. Our plans are specific actions we intend to take: "I plan to start my own business." Our path is the general direction of our daily lives: "I will seek to honor God in all I do." Our plans can change or even fail. But if we are on the right path, Proverbs says we will be okay. The path of life always leads upward for the prudent. This is an encouraging truth! King David had a plan to build a temple for God in Jerusalem. His plan never came to fruition. Yet, he is remembered not for this fruitless plan but as a man after God's own heart (Acts 13:22). Even when our plans are derailed, it does not mean we have failed as long as we are on the path of honoring God. Therefore, we should give even more thought and energy to our life path than to our life plans.

Lord, have I been so focused on my life plans that I have ignored the path of my life? Help me to give greater thought to who I am than what I do. Amen.

171

Do You Have a Plan to Get to Heaven?

Dave Freeman wrote the best-selling book *100 Things to Do Before You Die*. It included recommendations for all kinds of adventures, such as running with the bulls in Pamplona, Spain, and spending New Years' Eve in Times Square. Tragically, Freeman was able to accomplish only about half of the one hundred things in his book. He fell in his home in California and hit his head. He died at age forty-seven.[43] Death cuts short the plans of all of us.

Have you planned for your death? Death is the one certainty in life. It would be foolish to plan for things that may or may not happen (retirement, disability, fire, theft) and fail to plan for what is certain to happen (death). The Bible says that each of us will die and that each of us will face judgment after death (Hebrews 9:27). It would be foolish to plan for the seventy or eighty years of life on this earth and fail to plan for the eternity to follow. Your biggest life goal should be to go to heaven when you die. Do you have a plan to reach that goal?

Jesus said the only successful plan for getting to heaven is to follow him. Before he left earth, Jesus told his disciples, "I am going to prepare a place for you. You know the way (road or path) to the place where I am going."

One of them protested, "We don't know where you are going, so how can we know the way?"

Jesus responded, "I am the way and the truth and the life. No one comes to the Father except through me" (John 14:2–6). Jesus is the path to heaven. Is your life plan to follow Jesus?

> Lord Jesus, I want to go to heaven when I die. I know the only way to get there is to follow you now here on earth. I want to follow your path today. Amen.

God Is Sovereign over Our Plans

Proverbs tells us it is wise to plan ahead. Proverbs also reminds us that our plans will not always come to fruition. It is right for us to plan, but we must realize that the Lord may disrupt our plans to accomplish his purpose:

> Many are the plans in a man's heart,
> but it is the Lord's purpose that prevails. (Proverbs 19:21)

In November 1785, the Scottish poet Robert Burns was working in his field when he plowed up the nest of a field mouse. Burn wrote, *To a Mouse, on Turning Her Up in Her Nest with the Plough*. It reads in part:

> You saw the fields laid bare and wasted,
> And weary winter coming fast,
> And cozy here, beneath the blast,
> You thought to dwell,
> Till crash! the cruel plough passed
> Out through your cell.
>
> But little Mouse, you are not alone,
> In proving foresight may be vain:
> The best laid schemes of mice and men
> Go often askew,
> And leave us nothing but grief and pain,
> For promised joy!

Burns captured beautifully the feelings we have when our plans are crashed. However, Proverbs says we are not left with only grief and pain. We have a sovereign God who crashes our nests in order to plow a field that will yield a rich harvest.

> Lord, I tend to hurry around with my clock and my calendar as if I am in complete control. Today I humble myself beneath your sovereign hand. I acknowledge that you are God, and I am not. I thank you that you have a purpose greater than my little plans. Amen.

Be Willing to Change Your Plans

In their hearts humans plan their course,
but the LORD establishes their steps.
—Proverbs 16:9

This proverb should make us open to change. God may have a different plan for our day or our lives. The unexpected may be better than what we planned.

After Jesus died and was buried, some of his followers went to the tomb on the following Sunday morning. Their plan was to anoint Jesus's body with spices they had purchased, but the heavenly Father had raised Jesus from the dead. An angel told them to go tell the disciples that Jesus was alive. Their plans for the day were quickly changed.

On Paul's second missionary journey, he planned to go to Asia to preach, but the Holy Spirit did not allow him to follow his plan. His backup plan was to preach in Bithynia, but again the Spirit of Jesus prevented him from doing so. The only direction left was to go to the seaport of Troas. That night Paul had a vision of a man from Macedonia standing and begging, "Come over to Macedonia and help up." Luke wrote, "After Paul had seen the vision, we got ready at once to leave to Macedonia, concluding that God had called us to preach the gospel to them" (Acts 16:10).

Have you hit a brick wall with some of your plans? Rather than be dismayed, why not consider whether God is doing something different? Pause and take a step back. God may confirm your plans, and you will go forward again. Or God may move you in an unexpected and better direction.

> Sovereign Lord, today I will plan my course, but I recognize that
> you establish my steps. I want to be sensitive to your purposes even
> if it means changing my plans. Amen.

God Always Accomplishes His Purposes

To humans belong the plans of the heart,
but from the LORD comes the proper answer of the tongue.
—Proverbs 16:1

Humans make plans, but God is the one who determines what actually happens. This proverb reminds me of the story of the prophet Balaam in Numbers 22–24. The Israelites passed through Moab on their way from Egypt to the land of Canaan. The king of Moab was terrified by this horde of people passing through his land, so he hired Balaam to pronounce a curse on the Israelites. But when Balaam opened his mouth, he blessed them instead! "Balak said to Balaam, 'What have you done to me? I brought you to curse my enemies, but you have done nothing but bless them!'

He answered, 'Must I not speak what the Lord puts in my mouth?'" (Numbers 23:11–12). God always has the last word.

Perhaps you are frustrated and agitated today because some of your plans are not working out. An understanding of God's sovereignty can help relieve some of your anxiety. Your heavenly Father is in control. Take encouragement from the fact that he always has the last word.

> Father, I confess my anxiety about some of my plans. Quiet my heart and help me to rest in your sovereign control. Thank you, Lord. Amen.

God Can Direct Human Hearts Like a Stream of Water

In the LORD's hand the king's heart is a stream of water
that he channels toward all who please him.
—Proverbs 21:1

I have thought a lot about this verse, and I invite you to contemplate what it means. First, it gives me encouragement to know God is in ultimate control. As a farmer can guide water in an irrigation ditch, or a city can guide water in an aqueduct, so God can channel the hearts of world leaders to accomplish his purposes. God did this with Cyrus, king of Persia, when he directed Cyrus to release the Israelites from captivity in Babylon. That comforts me.

Then I wonder why God does not direct the king's heart more. Why doesn't he change the heart of North Korea's dictator? Why doesn't he change the hearts of Supreme Court justices when they rule against godly values and religious liberty? This is the question of the relationship between human freewill and divine sovereignty.

Perhaps the image of water helps. When you direct water in a waterway, you do so in accord with the direction it wants to go. Water wills to go downhill. You use that will to direct it where you desire. For example, Pharaoh wanted to oppose Moses, so God hardened his heart to accomplish his purpose of displaying his glory. Caesar Augustus wanted to tax his empire, so God used that will and channeled it to get Joseph back to Bethlehem. God certainly can work against human will, but usually he works with it to accomplish his purposes.

> Lord, I pray that you would direct our president's heart like a stream of water. I pray this for our leaders in Congress and in the judiciary. I pray that you will direct my heart like a stream of water to fulfill your purposes in my life. Amen.

No Plan Can Succeed Against the Lord

There is no wisdom, no insight, no plan
that can succeed against the LORD.
—Proverbs 21:30

Sometimes other people have evil plans for your life. Perhaps a coworker is plotting to make you look bad so he can get your position. Perhaps someone is spreading rumors about you in order to discredit you. On a national level, there are plots to disenfranchise Christians in the public schools, in academia, and in government. We can take comfort in the fact that no plan can ultimately succeed against the Lord. God can work even evil plans into his sovereign purposes.

The story of Joseph in Genesis 37–50 is an example of this proverb. Joseph's older brothers were jealous of him. They plotted to murder him and tell their father he was killed by a wild animal. Later they amended their plan and sold him as a slave to a caravan headed to Egypt. Joseph eventually gained his freedom and rose to power in Egypt. God revealed to him that a great famine was coming. Joseph was put in charge of the granaries of Egypt, where he stockpiled food to last through the famine. Eventually his brothers came to Egypt to buy grain to try to survive the famine. God used their evil plot as a way to provide for his chosen people during a time of trouble. When Joseph's brothers realized they were buying grain from their little brother whom they had betrayed, they were afraid. Joseph told them, "Don't be afraid. Am I in the place of God? You intended to harm me, but God intended it for good to accomplish what is now being done, the saving of many lives" (Genesis 50:19–20).

Sovereign Lord, you know the plans of my enemies. Edit their plans and change the storyline into one of blessing for me and your kingdom. Amen.

Do Your Best and Trust in the Lord

The horse is made ready for the day of battle,
but victory rests with the LORD.
—Proverbs 21:31

This proverb sums up the two themes about our plans and God's purposes. If you are going into battle, make sure your horse is ready, but realize that God is ultimately in control. It is wise to prepare and to plan ahead. It is also wise to cast yourself on God. Human effort and trust in God are complementary not contradictory.

Oliver Cromwell captured this combination when addressing his army during the invasion of Ireland. He said, "Put your trust in God, but keep your powder dry." He recognized that victory belonged to God, but he knew his men must be diligent to keep their gunpowder dry if they were to be successful. William Blacker immortalized these words in his poem *Oliver's Advice*. One stanza reads:

The Pow'r that led his chosen, by pillar'd cloud and flame,
Through parted sea and desert waste, that Pow'r is still the same.
He fails not—He, the loyal hearts that firm on him rely—
So put your trust in God, my boys, and keep your powder dry.

It does not show lack of faith in God to make good preparations. Plan your best. Then humbly submit your plans to God.

Lord, forgive me if I have failed to plan well. Forgive me also if I
have trusted in my plans and not in you. I resolve to do my best.
I resolve to put my hope completely in you. Amen.

Even Jesus Submitted His Will to the Father's Will

The night before he died, Jesus went through a genuine struggle with the sovereign purposes of the Father. He was deeply distressed and troubled, overwhelmed with sorrow to the point of death (Mark 14:33–34). As he prayed in anguish, his sweat was like drops of blood falling to the ground (Luke 22:44). Jesus prayed for an alternate plan. He shrank from the prospect of bearing the sins of the world. He prayed, "My Father, if it is possible, may this cup be taken from me. Yet not as I will, but as you will" (Matthew 26:39). That is an incredible verse! Jesus recognized that his will—his desires and hopes—did not in that moment match the will of the Father. Similarly, there will be times when our desires do not match the will of the Father.

Yet, in the end Jesus submitted to the Father's purpose, praying, "My Father, if it is not possible for this cup to be taken away unless I drink it, may your will be done" (Matthew 26:42). Jesus yielded his hopes to the sovereign purpose of the Father, and we are eternally blessed by his submission.

If Jesus had to let go of his desires, certainly there will be times when we have to do the same. Are you struggling to relinquish to God some of your hopes and dreams and plans? Can you believe that God's purposes might yield even greater blessings than your plans?

> Father, I yield my hopes and dreams to your sovereign purposes.
> I do not always understand your ways, but I trust your goodness.
> I will calm my heart and wait to see how you will bring blessing
> through my life. Amen.

A Review of the Five Megathemes of Proverbs

Proverbs 31:10–31

Proverbs ends with a poem describing a great wife. I used to think it was an odd way to end this book. But what better way to conclude a book addressed to young men than to talk about girls? Proverbs is advice to young men about wise choices. Guys, here is what you should look for and pray for in a girlfriend or wife. Girls, here is what you should look for in a husband, and here is the kind of woman God wants you to be. The qualities described in this poem should be the goals for your life.

More than just advice about a great wife, this poem is a deliberate review of the main themes of Proverbs. This chapter provides a summary of what it means to be a wise person, whether male or female, regardless of marital status or intention. This chapter is a review of the five big themes of Proverbs. This poem is a summary of how to live a wise life.

This poem is an acrostic. That is, each of the twenty-two verses begins with a successive letter in the Hebrew alphabet. (Psalm 119 and Lamentations 1–4 are other acrostic poems in the Bible.) This pattern aided memorization. The writer hoped that young men would internalize this advice about the five keys to a better life. It would be wise for us to memorize these five keys as well. We will count down this list of megathemes from number five to number one.

> Dear Lord, as I review the five megathemes of Proverbs this week,
> show me the areas in which I need to grow in order to become a
> person of wisdom. Amen.

A Great Wife Manages Money Well

A great wife works hard and shops wisely:

> She selects wool and flax and works with eager hands.
> She is like the merchant ships bringing her food from afar.
> (Proverbs 31:13–14)

She provides food for her family:

> She gets up while it is still night;
> she provides food for her family
> and portions for her female servants. (Proverbs 31:15)

She is a wise investor:

> She considers a field and buys it;
> out of her earnings she plants a vineyard. (Proverbs 31:16)

She is generous to the poor:

> She opens her arms to the poor
> and extends her hands to the needy. (Proverbs 31:20)

She strategically plans for the future:

> When it snows, she has no fear for her household;
> for all of them are clothed in scarlet. (Proverbs 31:21)

Money management is one of the biggest factors in the health of a marriage. It can be a source of stress and disagreement or it can unify a marriage if a couple works together for common goals and dreams. Money is the fifth biggest theme in Proverbs. If you want to have a better life, you need to follow God's principles of money management. If you want to choose a good spouse, look for someone who manages money well.

> Dear Lord, if your purposes for me include marriage, help me to choose wisely the person I will marry. Give me discernment. Help me to value the five qualities in this chapter in the same way that you value them. Amen.

A Great Wife Speaks with Wisdom

She speaks with wisdom,
and faithful instruction is on her tongue.
—Proverbs 31:26

A great wife is evidenced by how she talks. The second line of this proverb emphasizes that a great wife teaches her family about her faith and values.

The fourth biggest theme in Proverbs—and the fourth key to a better life—is your tongue, or how you talk to people. Proverbs says your words are a window into your heart. They reveal who you are on the inside. Do you want to know the content of your boyfriend's heart? Be quiet and listen. His words will tell you what is in his heart. If his words are profane, his heart is profane. If his words are often negative, critical, and demeaning of others, that will be his attitude in your relationship. If his conversation is self-centered, his life is also self-centered. Look for a partner who speaks with wisdom.

While you are listening, listen to yourself. How do you sound? What does your pattern of conversation reveal about your heart? A wise person speaks with wisdom.

Lord, I don't like some of the words that come out of my mouth.
I realize they indicate I have a heart problem. Change my heart,
Lord, and let this heart change begin to be reflected in a new way
of talking, a manner of conversation that honors you and benefits
me and those around me. Thank you, Lord. Amen.

A Great Wife Has Healthy Relationships

Her husband has full confidence in her
and lacks nothing of value.
She brings him good, not harm,
all the days of her life.
—Proverbs 31:11–12

Her children arise and call her blessed;
her husband also, and he praises her.
—Proverbs 31:28

A great wife has earned the trust and respect of her husband by her consistency and dependability in life. These are qualities you want to look for in a spouse as you contemplate marriage. How does your prospective mate relate to the people around her in other settings? Healthy relationships with family, friends, and coworkers are indicators of the potential for a healthy marriage relationship. A person who is continually in dysfunctional relationships may bring those same dynamics to the marriage relationship.

The third biggest theme in Proverbs—and the third most important key to a better life—is how you relate to other people. Your relationships can bring you joy or misery. Often we blame poor relationships on those around us: "I would relate to my relatives (or coworkers or neighbors) better if I had better relatives (or coworkers or neighbors)!" There could be some truth in that, but Proverbs calls us to look within ourselves at how we are cultivating the relationships around us.

Lord, rather than yearning for relationships I do not yet have, help me to become healthy in the relationships you have already given me. Help me to see that my current relationships are a training ground to prepare me for the future you have for me. Thank you, Lord, for working in my life through these relationships. Amen.

A Great Wife is a Person of Noble Character

A wife of noble character who can find?
She is worth far more than rubies.
—Proverbs 31:10

Guys, one of the wisest things you can do is find a spouse of moral character. She is worth more than rubies. The same could be said to girls. Look for and pray for a person of character. Don't settle for less. Settle for someone who bites her fingernails or who has a weird laugh but not for a person without character. Character produces trust in marriage.

In the Hebrew arrangement of the Bible, the book of Ruth follows the book of Proverbs. Ruth is an example of a woman of noble character (Ruth 3:11). She did not have everything going for her. She was poor. She was in a foreign country. But she was a person of character. Boaz recognized her character. They were soon married, and Ruth became part of the genealogy of Jesus Christ!

Character is a major concern of Proverbs. Righteousness is the second biggest theme in Proverbs. Proverbs contrasts the two ways of righteousness and wickedness. Of the six hundred proverbs in this book, one hundred of them contain one of these two words. In every area of life you have a choice between the right way and the wrong way to live. Character is the accumulation of your choices. If you choose to be promiscuous, you become a person of bad character. If you choose to cheat, you become a deceiver. If you choose righteousness, you become a person of noble character. To change your character, change your choices.

O Lord, give me a desire for righteousness greater than all other desires. Amen.

A Great Wife Fears the Lord

Charm is deceptive, and beauty is fleeting;
but a woman who fears the LORD is to be praised.
—Proverbs 31:30

The number one theme in Proverbs is wisdom. The number one key to wisdom is to fear the Lord. The fear of the Lord is the beginning of wisdom (Proverbs 9:10). Fear of the Lord is an awareness that God is holy and that we are accountable to him.

The most important thing to look for in a spouse is a person who fears the Lord. If your girlfriend does not fear God, no matter how charming or beautiful, dump her! (If you have already married a person who does not fear the Lord, that is another subject entirely. Keep your vow, and stick with that person. God can still bless your family. (See 1 Corinthians 7:10–16). Spiritual reverence and moral character are the two most important qualities in a spouse. Make these nonnegotiable in your search for a marriage partner.

Solomon spoke most of the proverbs in this book (Proverbs 1:1). But the last chapter contains the sayings of another king, King Lemuel, who is otherwise unknown to us (Proverbs 31:1). Why does the book end with words from a different king? Solomon failed in this area of his life. Solomon was the wisest man who ever lived (1 Kings 10:23–24), but he did not follow God's advice about choosing a great wife. He chose a wife who did not fear the Lord and who did not have great character (1 Kings 11:1–4). Solomon suffered because of his choice. God was angry with him and took part of his kingdom away from Solomon's descendants.

> O Lord, above everything else in my prayers, I pray that I may stand in awe of you. If marriage is in my future, guide me to a person who shares this reverence for you. Thank you, Lord. In Jesus's name I pray. Amen.

How Can I Do All This Stuff?

Proverbs 31 describes a great wife, an ideal wife, maybe even a perfect wife. This chapter can be intimidating. You may read these characteristics of a great wife/wise person and find them overwhelming and exhausting. The same could be said about the entire book of Proverbs. The role of Proverbs is to show us the right way in life, the way of wisdom. It gives us a blueprint for a better life, but it leaves us without a building contractor.

The New Testament adds two more dimensions to the picture of a better life. First, the New Testament tells us that when we fail to follow the way of wisdom, God still loves us. We have all failed. We have all turned to our own way. What we need even more than a blueprint is a Savior. So God sent us his Son, Jesus, to save us from our mistakes. "For God did not send his Son into the world to condemn the world, but to save the world through him" (John 3:17). God extends grace to us and offers to forgive us through Jesus.

Second, the New Testament offers us an inner power that enables us to follow the way of wisdom. When we receive Jesus as our Savior, the Father sends the Spirit of Jesus into our lives to guide us and empower us. The Spirit of truth keeps us on the way of wisdom. "Walk by the Spirit, and you will not gratify the desires of the flesh" (Galatians 5:16).

> Dear Lord, I have not always chosen the path of wisdom in my life. Thank you for loving me in spite of my rebellion. I am amazed that you want to forgive me. I want your presence and help in my life. Thank you for sending your Son, Jesus, to save me. I confess Jesus as my Savior and Lord. Jesus, thank you for putting your Spirit in my life. Holy Spirit, teach me truth, guide my steps, and empower my will to follow the way of wisdom. In Jesus's name I pray. Amen.

Conclusion

So, what do you think? Is your life better now than it was 175 days ago? If you have put these principles of wisdom into practice, I am betting that you have seen some immediate improvement in your life. God knows how life should work! He designed us, and we live better lives when we follow his plan for us.

There are two things to keep in mind. First, this does not mean that your circumstances have improved. You may have lost your job or gotten sick during these last six months. You may have ended an unhealthy relationship, and that may have caused you some stress. Wisdom does not guarantee you will have better circumstances, but it guarantees you will become a better person. In fact, God may be using some adverse circumstances to refine you and further strengthen some of the wise principles you have learned.

Second, keep in mind that spiritual growth is a process that takes time: "First the stalk, then the head, then the full kernel in the head" (Mark 4:28). While you have probably seen some immediate results from following the wisdom of Proverbs, the full fruit of your obedience to God will richly manifest itself in the months, years, and even decades to come if you will stay on course! Satan will try to discourage you and distract you from the way of wisdom. He wants to rob you of the gains you have made. Don't give up. Remember, "For though the righteous fall seven times, they rise again, but the wicked stumble when calamity strikes" (Proverbs 24:16). (That's the last proverb, I promise!)

Where do you go from here? If the wisdom of Proverbs was new to you, you may want to turn to the front of this book and start through it again! If you are ready to move on, find another daily devotional guide that is rooted in God's Word. May the way of wisdom lead you into a better life!

Scripture Index

Titus

Hebrews

James

1 Peter

Revelation

Endnotes

1   John Maxwell, *Falling Forward* (Nashville, TN: Thomas Nelson, 2000), 140.

2   Nancy C. Anderson, *Avoiding the Greener Grass Syndrome: How to Grow Affair-Proof Hedges Around Your Marriage* (Grand Rapids, MI: Kregel, 2004), 88–95.

3   David Lodge, "Afterword," in *The British Museum Is Falling Down* (London: Vintage, 2011), 171.

4   C. S. Lewis, *Mere Christianity* (New York: Macmillian, 1952), 17.

5   John C. Maxwell, *Failing Forward* (Nashville: Thomas Nelson, 2000), 173–74.

6   Uniform Crime Report, www.ucr.fbi.gov/crime-in-the-u.s.

7   Global Retail Theft Barometer Study, www.market.com/story (Published November 6, 2014).

8   Insurance Fraud, www.fbi.gov/stats-services/publications/insurance-fraud.

9   Federal Tax Compliance Research: Tax Gap Estimates for Tax Years 2008-2010 (May 2016), www.irs.gov/uac/irs-the-tax-gap.

10 Theodore Roosevelt, "The Strenuous Life," a speech given in Chicago, April 10, 1899, published in *Outlook,* May 12, 1890.

11 Tamar Lewin, "Dean at MIT Resigns, Ending a 28-Year Lie," *New York Times,* April 27, 2007.

12 "Alcohol, Drugs, and Crime", National Association of Alcoholism and Drug Dependence, www.ncadd.org/about-addiction (June 27, 2015).

13 Henry Wechsler, George Kuh, Andrea E. Davenport, "Fraternities, Sororities and Binge Drinking: Results from a National Study of American Colleges," *NASPA Journal* 46, no. 3 (2009): 395–416.

14 Sue McClure, "Driver Shoots Car after It Quits on Him," *Tennessean,* March 10, 2013.

15 *Fort Worth Star-Telegram,* September 6, 1986.

16 Sherrie Bourg Carter, "Emotions Are Contagious—Choose Your Company Wisely," www.psychologytoday.com, posted October 20, 2012.

17 Stephen E. Ambrose, *Eisenhower: Soldier and President* (New York: Simon and Schuster, 1990), 18–19.

18 www.whitehousegifts.com/pages/the-presidential-seal-a-brief-history.

19 Ned Zeman, "The Man Who Loved Grizzlies," *Vanity Fair,* May 2004, www.vanityfair.com/news/2004/05/timothy-treadwell.

20 Christopher Reeve, *Still Me* (New York: Random House, 1998).

21 "Urban Meyer Will Be Home for Dinner," *ESPN the Magazine,* August 2012, 107–18.

22 Quoted by Carolyn Arends, "Wrestling with Angels," *Christianity Today,* April 2013, 60.

23 Joy Allmond, "A Commitment to Put Christ First," *Decision*, May 2016, 2.

24 Howard G. Hendricks. AZQuotes.com. Wind and Fly LTD, 2017. Accessed April 6, 2017.

25 William J. Reynolds, *Companion to the Baptist Hymnal* (Nashville: Broadman Press, 1978), 238.

26 Barbara Johnson, *Stick a Geranium in Your Hat and Be Happy* (Nashville: Thomas Nelson, 2004).

27 Hara Estroff Marano, "Depression Doing the Thinking," *Psychology Today* (July 1, 2001), www.psychologytoday.com/articles/200107/depression-doing-the-thinking.

28 Wyatt Myers, "Depression: How to Challenge Negative Thinking," www.everydayhealth.com/hs/major-depression/how-to-challenge-negative-thinking-from-depression.

29 Adam Hoffman, "Are Positive Emotions Good for Your Heart?" www.greatergood.berkeley.edu.

30 Edward T. Creagan, "Going the Distance: Your Attitude Affects Your Reality," www.mayoclinic.org/healthy-lifestyle/stress-management.

31 William J. Reynolds, *Companion to the Baptist Hymnal* (Nashville: Broadman Press, 1976), 221.

32 Bernard Rimland, "The Altruism Paradox," *Psychological Reports* 51 (1982): 521.

33 www.loc.gov/exhibits/treasures/trm012.html.

34 Brenton Cox, *A Year in the Psalms* (Bloomington, IN: Crossbooks, 2010).

35 Bruce Waltke, *The Book of Proverbs, Chapters 15-31, New International Commentary on the Old Testament* (Grand Rapids, MI: William B. Eerdmans, 2005), 64.

36 "Study Finds No Difference in the Amount Men and Women Talk," Undergraduate Biology Research Program, www.uprb.arizona.edu.

37 David Jeremiah, *Hopeful Parenting* (Colorado Springs: David C. Cook, 2008), 234.

38 William M. Pinson Jr. comp., *An Approach to Christian Ethics: The Life, Contribution, and Thought of T. B. Maston* (Nashville, TN: Broadman Press, 1979), 65.

39 Ben Popken, "Poor People Spend 9% of Income on Lottery Tickets," www.consumerist.com, posted May 26, 2010.

40 Michael Tanner and Charles Hughes, "The Work Verses Welfare Tradeoff: 2013," Cato Institute, www.cato.org.

41 Jessica Dickler, "Most Americans Can't Afford a $1000 Emergency Expense," CNN Money, accessed July 22, 2015.

42 Bruce Wydick, "Want to Change the World? Sponsor a Child," *Christianity Today,* June 2013, 20.

43 "'100 Things' co-author Dave Freeman dies," www.dailynews.com, posted August 2008.